GROWING UP SAVED

A Tyndale nonfiction imprint

From hilarious chapter titles to heartbreaking stories, Kristen LaValley exposes the pain of growing up evangelical and the promise of being loved no matter what. A book brimming with kindness, honesty, and humor—*Growing Up Saved* is a refreshing read from a voice I respect.

K.J. RAMSEY

Therapist and author of *The Place Between Our Pains* and *The Book of Common Courage*

The American evangelical church is in crisis—shaped by power and defined more by fear than freedom. Many of the most sincere believers have found no balm for their spiritual, mental, or emotional pain. With unflinching personal honesty and thorough research, Kristen LaValley offers an inspiring, practical, Jesus-centered path forward for those who hunger for wholeness and integrity. As someone who has witnessed both the profound cost of spiritual abuse and the real power of Christ's living church, I am grateful for voices like Kristen's—truthful, kind, and rooted in grace.

JONATHAN PUDDLE

Pastor and author of *You Are Enough: Learning to Love Yourself the Way God Loves You*

Growing Up Saved is a raw and honest look at the struggles many face in the church, from self-doubt to perfectionism. Kristen's journey will resonate with anyone who has ever felt like they had to earn God's approval. With vulnerability and humor, Kristen invites us to stop hiding, stop performing, and rest in the truth that we are already loved. If you've ever questioned your faith or struggled to feel enough, this book will remind you that you're not alone and that God's love is far bigger than you've been told.

TONY MILTENBERGER
Host of the *Follow 2 Lead* podcast and author of *Wisdom in the Wound*

It's possible for someone to tell their story in such a way that, though it's wholly unique to them, it also becomes, somehow, universal. It's now for all of us. We find ourselves in the same rooms, at the same tables, wrestling the same issues, all because of their specific story. *Growing Up Saved* does that for us. Kristen's honesty and craftsmanship invite you in. Her insights and depth offer you hope. If you've ever wondered if life with God was really supposed to be heavy or if there was something better on offer, this book is for you.

MEREDITH MILLER
Pastor, speaker, and author of *Woven: Nurturing a Faith Your Kid Doesn't Have to Heal From*

Kristen LaValley

growing up saved

WHEN LOVING GOD
FEELS LIKE
LOSING YOURSELF

Visit Tyndale online at tyndale.com.

Visit Tyndale Momentum online at tyndalemomentum.com.

Visit the author online at kristenlavalley.com.

Growing Up Saved: When Loving God Feels Like Losing Yourself

Cover design by Julie Chen

Interior design by Cathy Miller

Edited by Stephanie Rische

The author is represented by Alive Literary Agency, www.aliveliterary.com.

For information about special discounts for bulk purchases, please contact Tyndale House Publishers at csresponse@tyndale.com, or call 1-855-277-9400.

Library of Congress Cataloging-in-Publication Data

A catalog record for this book is available from the Library of Congress.

ISBN 978-1-4964-7856-6

Printed in the United States of America

32 31 30 29 28 27 26
7 6 5 4 3 2 1

For the Jesus freaks
(former and current)

Before You Begin

IF YOU, LIKE ME, GREW UP SAVED in the '90s and early 2000s, you might recognize a few familiar phrases in the chapter titles. They're tongue-in-cheek nods to the culture that raised me, but that's not really what this book is about. If altar calls, rapture prep, and martyrdom drills weren't a part of your spiritual upbringing, don't worry. You don't need that background to find your way through these pages. But if you *do* catch the references, welcome. You're in good (slightly traumatized) company.

Another thing to note before you begin is that telling the truth—the whole truth—can be dangerous. The stories in this book are drawn from my real life, shaped by memory and meaning. But in a few places, I've changed some details to protect my family's safety and my own. If telling the truth didn't come with consequences, some parts of this book would read quite differently—and I suspect you'll know which ones. These are the stories I can tell without losing more than I already have. I hope that the shadows and echoes of what really happened will outline the shape of a wound that has long since healed over.

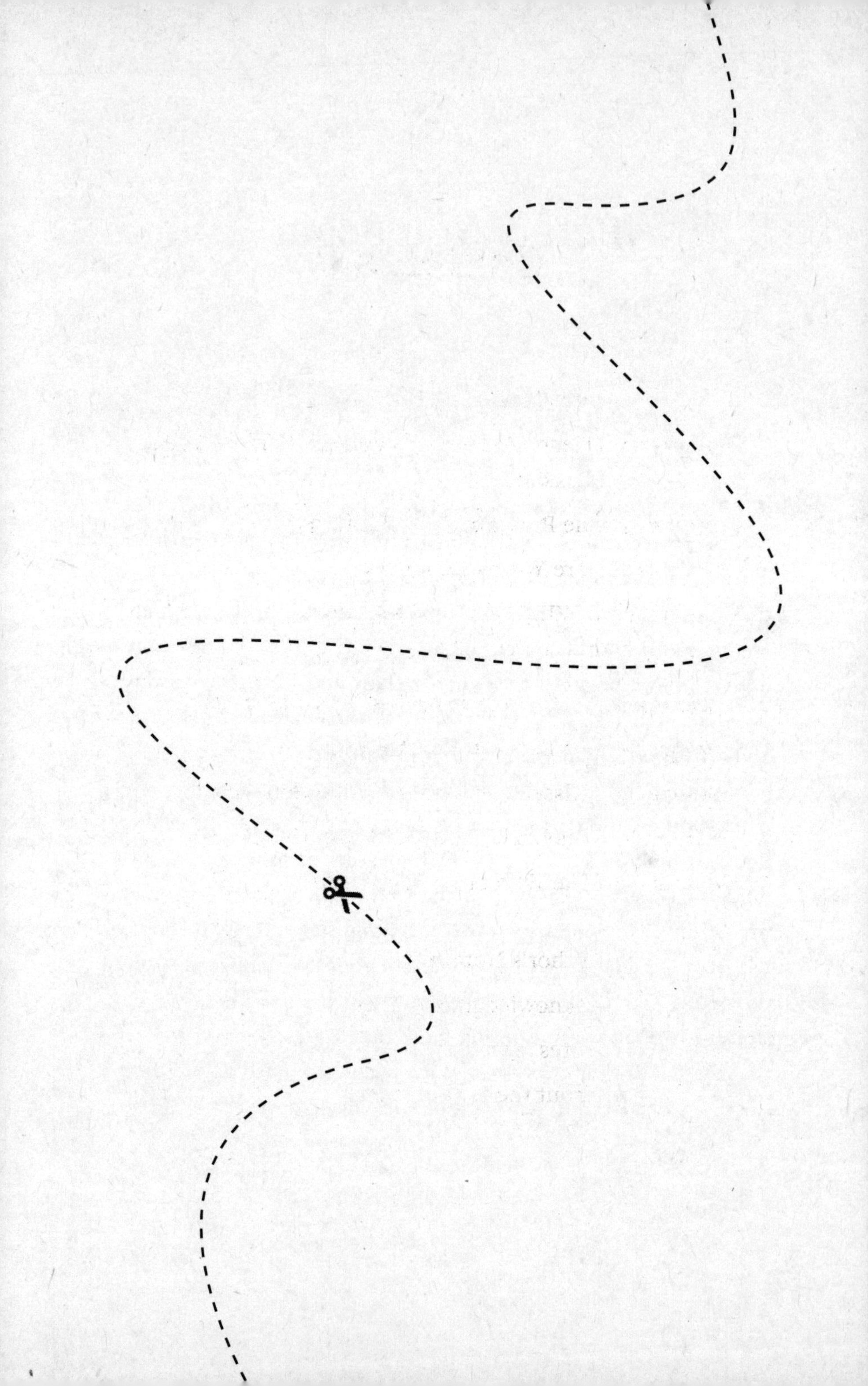

Contents

Introduction

I'M THREE YEARS OLD, sitting on the stairs at my aunt's house during a family gathering. I've just said something funny, and my aunt takes out her camcorder to have me say it again.

"Tell me what you said again, Kristen. Where is Jesus?"

I kick my little legs and respond, "Jethus ith in mah haht and he bit my tongue."

Everyone laughs. I run off to play. I'm barely potty-trained, but I've just made a confession of faith.

I'm five years old, sitting in the front seat of my mom's car, turning onto Holly Drive, Nana and Papa's street. This will become one of my earliest memories. I say a quiet prayer in my head and turn to my mom and say, "I just asked Jesus in my heart!"

She smiles and says, "That's great, Kristen!"

I'm fifteen years old. Last week I got caught at the mall with a boy I met in a chat room. Dad spanked me, and I'm grounded from prom and for life. I'm cleaning my room, and I find my *Extreme Teen Bible* under my bed and throw it.

Later that day, I find the tossed Bible lying open in a corner. I pick it up and glance at the devotion on the page: "Be encouraged! It doesn't matter what you've done in the past, where you've done it, or who you've done it with. God loves you and wants to forgive you."

I start crying. "Okay, Jesus. I'll follow you now."

I'm thirty years old. My husband, my kids, and I have just been pushed out of a church we love. I'm sad, angry, lonely, and scared. I'm not sure if anything I've believed until now is true anymore. I'm terrified of what that could mean for me. I write in my journal, "Have you ever loved me? Have I ever been worthy of your love? I'm not sure anymore. Maybe your promises weren't for me."

I'm approaching forty years old. My faith has unraveled in ways I never could have imagined at three, five, fifteen, or thirty. My journey with Christ has been complicated, frustrating, and beautiful. I have held on through mental health crises, traumas, and a late-in-life ADHD diagnosis. And somehow I have come to peace—not the kind of peace I once chased through self-denial and spiritual striving, but peace with myself, and in that, peace with Christ.

I have spent most of my life thinking God was disappointed in me. Many nights in my childhood were spent lying awake, listing every tiny thing I'd done "wrong" that day, just in case Jesus came back or I died in my sleep. Every breath I took felt like a threat to my eternal life, so I prayed my whole self away. I didn't just *think* I was bad; I felt it deep in my bones. I don't mean that in the general, fallen-world "we all sin and fall short" kind of way. I mean deep, personal, existential disappointment. I believed my very existence made God sigh. I grew up believing that holiness guaranteed you a life without struggle and that righteousness meant suppressing anything inconvenient or undesirable about yourself. I thought that if I prayed hard enough, disciplined myself enough, denied myself enough, I could finally become the kind of person God wanted me to be. I have journal pages filled with prayers begging God to change me.

> Why did you make me this way?
> Please break me and make me more like you.
> I'm sorry I'm not good.

I didn't realize then that the things I was begging God to change weren't my "sin nature." They were who I was—a reflection of the image of God in me. But because I had been formed in a faith framework where holiness was just as much about what could be perceived as it was a posture of the heart, I saw my uniqueness—my struggles, my emotions, even the way my brain worked—as barriers to being loved by God.

I spent years trying to break myself into pieces, attempting to get away from things that were just . . . me. I read the books. I attended the conferences. I rededicated my life at altar calls over and over again. I did my best to mold myself into the kind of person who would finally feel at home in her own skin. But instead of making me holy, it made me miserable. I hated myself, but I thought that was a virtue. I thought self-loathing was the appropriate response to a holy God.

That self-hatred had consequences. It affected my ability to form healthy friendships. It made me believe that love was something I had to earn. It made me anxious, obsessive, starved for approval. And eventually, when I couldn't hold it all together anymore, that self-hatred turned outward—toward the only one I thought I could blame. God.

When sin entered the world, it didn't just break our relationship with God—it broke *everything*. It fractured our relationships, our sense of safety, even our connection to ourselves. We inherited shame, and that shame has made us hide ever since. And yet, when Adam and Eve hid, God searched for them. "Where are you?" he asked. He wasn't disgusted by their nakedness. He didn't withdraw his love. He went looking for them.

For years, I believed that freedom meant perfection. That to be free in Christ meant to be free from my struggles, my doubts, my complexities. That once I arrived at some mythical level of spiritual maturity, I would finally feel loved and at peace. But that's not freedom. That's a trap. Real freedom—the kind Christ has given me—is the freedom to stop hiding. To stop pretending. To stop performing. To let go of the exhausting work of being acceptable and instead rest in the truth that I already am accepted.

I no longer believe that my struggles disqualify me from grace. I no longer believe that my identity is wrapped up in whether I get everything right. I no longer believe that God is standing over me with a cosmic clipboard, evaluating my worth. I no longer live my life flinching, waiting for divine punishment. I am free because I know who I am—loved, held, forgiven, covered, and safe.

I've danced at altars and left the church. I've led worship and removed worship playlists from my phone. I've spoken to large crowds about the goodness of God, and I've shaken my fist at the sky and declared God a jerk. My faith has bent and broken and unraveled, and yet in my weakest moments, I have breathed a prayer: *Where else would I go?*

Faith isn't as linear as we might have thought.

I guess there are a few places I could go. Many have traveled this road before me and with me and have ended up at different destinations. Faith, as it turns out, isn't as linear as we might have thought. For a child, it's simple: "Ask Jesus into your heart, and you'll be saved." For an adult, it's a bit more complicated. When our deeply held beliefs can't comfort our traumas, our grief, and our doubts, we struggle to reconcile what we thought were spiritual guarantees with the reality we're living in. For most of us, belief is a decision that happens many times over the course of a lifetime.

A few years after we left our last ministry position, heartbroken and disoriented, I found myself in an unexpected ministry walking with people who have been hurt by the church, have experienced some kind of faith-altering trauma, or have become disillusioned with their faith. In private messages, Zoom calls, writing courses, retreats, "chance" meetings with strangers, or scheduled cups of coffee, I have been a witness to stories of pain and trauma that have gone long unheard. Because of what I've seen, held, and carried, I've become a fierce defender of the deconstructed, the wounded, and the *done*.

I've watched people desperately try to cling to the faith they once knew, even as it fell apart in their hands. I've held them as their trauma collided with tightly built frameworks, shattering what once felt sure. I've helped them connect with resources and communities—sometimes to leave abusive relationships, sometimes to find safety outside the grip of leaders who use their authority to manipulate and control. I've wept with them as they tried to make sense of a God they were told loves them, and heal from the harm done to them in his name.

Almost ten years and hundreds of people later, it's clear that no one steps into this kind of pain and unraveling willingly. They are catapulted into it, alone and afraid, not turning their backs on God but begging him to throw them a rope. They're just trying to find a way to hold on to him when nothing they've been taught about him feels true anymore.

I see them. I know them. I *am* them. I found my way to Jesus with both pain and disillusionment in hand. He welcomed me. So did his people. So now I do the same thing for others. How could I do anything else?

Maybe you've spent your life feeling like something in you is intrinsically broken. Maybe you've never felt like you are enough. Maybe you were taught that God's love is conditional, that you need to get your act together before you can be embraced. Maybe you're still carrying the weight of a faith that was formed in fear.

I want you to know this:

You are loved by God.

You are also *liked* by him.

And it has nothing to do with what you have or haven't done—it has everything to do with who he is.

God isn't waiting for you to become someone else. He isn't holding back his love until you reach some unattainable spiritual milestone. You don't have to earn it. You don't have to perform for it. You don't have to prove you deserve it. You don't have to contort yourself into the shape of someone holier, quieter, or more certain. You're already his. That's the radical love of Christ—the kind that doesn't flinch at doubt, at failure, at the slow unraveling of all the things you used to be sure about. It's the kind of love that holds steady when everything you thought you knew about God, yourself, and your faith starts to come undone.

Many of us who grew up saved have to unlearn the weight of

striving, the fear of getting things wrong, the exhaustion of trying to lift the heavy weight that bad theology and misunderstandings put around our necks. We have to relearn what God's love really is—not the version handed down to us, but the true love of God that sets us free.

Wherever you are on your journey with faith—whether you grew up saved like me or found Jesus somewhere else on the timeline of your life—I think you'll find pieces of your story in the tapestry of mine. This book is about the undoing and rebuilding of faith and identity. It's about finding God, maybe for the first time, in the spaces where we thought we were alone.

If you find yourself in my story, I hope my words are a lighthouse for you—not the soft, sentimental kind, but the kind that cuts through fog and panic and says, "You're not alone. You're almost there." It's a flare from someone who's been adrift too—someone who has questioned everything, walked away, come undone, and slowly stitched herself back together. And if some small part of you still dares to hope that life can be beautiful after heartbreak, that maybe God doesn't flinch at your existence, and that faith can feel like a deep breath instead of a burden, these words are for you. Let's find the shore together.

You don't have to contort yourself into the shape of someone holier, quieter, or more certain to be accepted by God. You're already his.

1

Friends Are Friends Forever (Unless You Backslide)

When Belonging Becomes Conditional

MARIE TERRACE, MILLTOWN, NEW JERSEY, 1996

I'M SITTING ON MY KNEES on the floor of my living room with my older brother Christopher and my little brother Jonathan on either side of me. Mom sits my little sister Abby, who just had her first birthday, on the couch next to her and picks up my newborn baby brother Zachary from his baby seat to give him a bottle. Dad's here, but he isn't, really. He sits on the chair in the corner of the room, quiet and still.

Jonathan is only five, so he's fidgety and silly and keeps asking questions that have nothing to do with what my older brother and I have recognized is a serious family meeting. We exchange looks but don't speak. Last night, Christopher pulled me into his room and told me that something bad was happening at church and that we needed to be good so we wouldn't add any more stress to Mom and Dad. We're only eleven and nine, but we know something isn't right.

Mom takes a deep breath and closes her eyes. "I have to tell you guys something. We won't be going back to church this Sunday. Dad doesn't work there anymore."

I catch my breath. Christopher freezes. Jonathan wails, "What? Why?"

Mom exhales.

"Why, Mom?" I ask.

"Some of the people at church decided they don't want him to be the pastor anymore. We can never go there again."

My heart is racing. "What about Sara? Suzanne? Gia?" I'm only thinking of what this means for me. The church is my whole world. My family. My school. My friends. I don't have a life outside of it. I can feel something shift in Christopher next to me. The air around him changes, and his shoulders straighten. He's asking thoughtful questions, suppressing his own fear and confusion because he recognizes what I can't yet: Our mother is heartbroken.

Jonathan is crying now and asks the question that's most important to him—a question so innocent, so achingly sincere that it slices through the heaviness in the room: "Will we get to bring our refrigerator with us when we move?"

Mom laughs, and a few tears fall down her cheeks.

I don't understand much of what's going on. But I know enough to know that everything is going to change.

In case you're wondering, no. We didn't take the fridge with us. We did, however, pack up a nice starter kit of unresolved grief, trust issues, and relational trauma. As it turns out, when your life collapses, it doesn't always come with a tidy emotional timeline.

Some things take time to process, but eventually you start to realize where the fracture happened.

There are moments in your life that become a dividing line. Everything after The Event is the *anno Domini*. All it takes is one giant wrecking ball to split your life into two sections: before that day and after that day. For me, there was "before East Brunswick" and "after East Brunswick."

This isn't just a metaphor, it's how we talk about things in my family. It serves as a verbal shortcut, packed with meaning that doesn't need unpacking, to contextualize our lives. "Well, after East Brunswick . . ." No one needs to mention specifics. The statement alone is packed with meaning and implication—everyone in the conversation knows exactly what it means. "East Brunswick" carries a heavy weight in our family lore.

My dad had been pastoring a church in East Brunswick, New Jersey, for a few years. This church was supposed to be *it* for my parents. The last stop. The place they'd stay. Their Camelot. They'd grow old and we'd grow up, and it would be good.

When my mom sat us down for a family meeting, she'd just given birth to my little brother, her fifth child. I didn't know she'd gone into labor early because of the trauma she'd just endured at the hands of the church they served. I didn't know about the creepy phone calls or why we'd gotten a fancy new caller ID attached to our phone. That night on the living room floor, I didn't know I was sitting in a fraction of the darkness my parents had been living in for months.

All I knew was what they told us.

In the days following that family meeting, Mom explained what happened in terms we could understand. You can't really tell a child, "There was a coup against your father," so what she told us was, "The board decided they don't like Dad anymore." They put him on trial in front of the whole church and accused him of all kinds of things—all of which were untrue, but the truth didn't matter.

My dad sat on the platform of the church—the same platform he'd stood on and preached from every Sunday—in front of his congregation, his staff, and the officials in charge of our regional denomination, and listened as they blindsided him with accusations. He was stealing money, they said. The treasurer stood up and said he wasn't. He cared more about the toilets in the church than the people, they said. My dad *did* care about the cleanliness of the toilets more than the average pastor, but even at nine years old, I knew that was a bit of a stretch. One by one, the accusations came. The ones that could be factually proven or disproven were. The ones that were subjective hung in the air and cast a dark shadow over everything that had once been good.

Everyone chose sides. Some were in support of the mutiny against my father. Some were against it and spoke up. Some were against it and stayed quiet, but there are no passive participants in injustice. There's no neutral. Even those who didn't choose a side made a choice. My mom, pregnant as could be, sat helplessly in a pew next to her mother as her husband was torn to shreds. At the end of the trial, one of the district officials said to my dad, "Take your family and get out as fast as you can."

A few hours later, my mom was in the hospital delivering my little brother, several weeks early. My older brother and I processed this event for years. We brought it up all the time, asking more and more questions as we got older, forcing my parents to reprocess their trauma with us over and over again. I like to think of it as intergenerational healing, but they'd probably call it harassment.

We just wanted to make sense of it, and as we matured, so did our understanding of what happened. But that day, sitting on the floor of our home that the church owned, all we understood was that our parents were sad and we weren't going back to our church, our school, or our friends.

Over the next several weeks, our phone rang nonstop. Everyone wanted to talk to my parents, to find out what happened, to offer their support, to get the real story. But there were also harassing phone calls, demands for us to leave our house, threats, heavy mouth-breathing on the other end of the line. My parents taught us to wait until the caller ID revealed who the caller was before answering. Of course, I didn't really know why we were doing all that. My dad was always an early adopter of new technology, so I'm sure I just thought it was one of his new gadgets.

I couldn't have known the psychological torture my mom and dad were enduring. All I knew was that overnight, everything I knew outside my home was gone and my mom was sad and my dad was angry. Everything in my life had revolved around our church, and then it didn't anymore. I just woke up one day and everything in my life was different.

"Different" has a way of quietly rearranging everything inside you. Friendship is important for all genders and all ages, but we can probably all agree that for nine-year-old girls, friendship is more important than, say, *breathing*. There are studies upon studies that show friendship at that stage is a critical part of identity development. It helps kids feel like they belong somewhere, like they're okay. It teaches them how to handle stress and helps them grow into their emotional and social selves.[1] There I was, at nine years old, stripped of contact with every friend, with little capacity to understand what was happening.

I didn't really feel the magnitude of the loss until one day in the first weeks after my dad was forced to resign from his position. I wasn't old enough to connect what was going on with my dad with the people who were our friends there. I hadn't talked to my best friend in a few weeks, so I decided to pick up the phone and give her a call.* As I was punching the last number into the phone, my mom must have sensed it, as moms tend to do, and she came running into the kitchen. She grabbed the phone and slammed it back on the receiver, and for the rest of my life, I'll remember the look on her face in that moment. Her eyes were wide, her eyebrows raised, her face pale. She was out of breath as if she'd just stopped me from running in front of a moving train. I was stunned and confused as I looked at her, both of her hands braced on the kitchen counter, tired eyes narrowed at me as she shook her head.

"We can't call anyone right now, Kristen," she said desperately. "We don't know who our friends are."

And I guess that's when everything really changed for me. That's when the ceiling cracked, and everything I'd had before that moment became just a sad memory. That's the moment that colored everything in my life moving forward and cast a shadow over everything that had come before. Because when you're nine, and you've never been through anything hard, and you don't have the emotional maturity to understand betrayal and people not liking your mom and dad, and your world revolves around your

* You might wonder why I would do this when we were already screening calls. Yes, I should've known better. But as you'll learn later, little Kristen had a bit of a "deficit of attention" problem.

friends, being told that you don't know who your friends are anymore shifts something big and important inside you.

That was the day I changed. I'd never be wide-eyed and naively accepting of people again. I would always side-eye, question, and doubt. I would forever choose exactly how much I'd give of myself and keep the rest of me to myself.

The church had betrayed me. It had broken my parents' hearts. It derailed my life. And although I didn't have the maturity to piece all these things together at that age, a narrative was being written in stone inside me: *The church cannot be trusted.*

My mom's simple explanation for why I couldn't call my friend formed itself into a core belief. "We don't know who our friends are" was an absolute, indisputable truth for me after that point. I believed that if I kept people out, I would stay safe. But constantly questioning the intentions and motives of the people in your life does more to keep *you* out, and as it turns out, it doesn't really do much to ward off pain. Even if you build up walls, people still find their way in through the cracks, and once they're in, they can break your heart.

Sometimes you just won't know who your friends are.

Friendship in spiritual communities can give an illusion of strength and depth. The intimacy that happens within the church gives us a false sense of relational and emotional safety. It feels safe because we all love Jesus, right? We can't imagine hurting each other. There's no way the people we break bread with would ever betray us or wound us so deeply we can't get out of bed. (Ahem. Jesus and Judas would like a word.) It's like living in a gated neighborhood, where we walk around saying, "That bad thing that happened in that other place would never happen here." We rationalize the spiritual abuse or relational splits that happen in other churches and speculate on why they happened. We think if we can understand why something happened, it will vaccinate us against the pain and trauma we've perceived but haven't experienced.

But what happens when our knowledge doesn't protect us? What do we do when our belonging becomes conditional? What if the security of our community is ripped away from us the moment we ask the wrong question, we challenge the wrong tradition, or we confess to the wrong struggle? If our acceptance in a spiritual community hinges on conformity, not connection—on following certain unspoken rules, on saying all the right things and believing all the right things, on keeping our doubts and fears tucked away so they don't make anyone else uncomfortable—that community is not a reflection of the body or character of Christ. If you find yourself in a space like that, exit through the side door. Belonging should not have to be earned.

Healing comes when the church is willing to make eye contact with your pain instead of being afraid of it.

When we're hurt in places that should be refuges for us, we metabolize the belief that community is conditional. Because it kind of is. Or at least that's what our experience has been and because of that, our faith is shaped by our fear of being cast out, rather than our transformation in Christ.

True community—the kind God intends for us—doesn't have neighborhood watchdogs policing behavior and determining who's on the list to get in or out. The church should be built on love, not control. Your community should be safe enough for you to be together, knowing full well that you're capable of hurting each other but choosing to stay, mend what's broken, and care for one another . . . and so fulfill the law of Christ (Galatians 6:2).

When we assume church is a safe place, we tend to open up with abandon and share intimate parts of ourselves with people, even when we barely know them. We immerse ourselves in each other's lives. We welcome strangers into our homes and into the lives of our spouses and our children. Caution is treated as cynicism—a trait that is widely considered un-Christlike. If you want to assimilate into a community, be open, be friendly, be hospitable, be extroverted, and for goodness' sake, put your guard down.

But being guarded isn't a flaw rooted in sin or cynicism. It's a protective, defensive position that we take when something has happened to make us feel unsafe. We come into this world wide-eyed and looking for love and protection. When we're rejected, mistreated, or neglected, we learn to protect ourselves. This is a good thing, wired into us by the one who made us. It's an instinct that helps us survive.

No one wants to get hurt in the same way twice, so we learn, whether consciously or subconsciously, to protect ourselves. The only way to heal from the pain that causes these defensive responses is to go through a process of repair. To repair relational wounds, we need healers. To find healers, we need to be in community. But how can we heal without returning to the place where we were harmed?

The question of how to heal after harm is one that has been asked often in recent years. There's been a broad conversation in evangelical spaces about pain that happens in and because of the church.

For a while, we called it *church hurt*. That phrase has been used as sort of a blanket term for any pain that happens in a church community. I'd like to make a distinction between *church hurt* and *spiritual trauma*.

Church hurt is an event that happens. This could be anything, big or small, that causes a person pain inside a faith community because of something that happened within that community. It could be caused by a pastor, a board, another church member, a teaching, or a church split. Spiritual trauma is the wound that's caused by such an event. If it helps, think of it like this: Church hurt is the cause; trauma is the effect. They're connected, but not the same. Not everyone who has been hurt in the church has trauma, but everyone who has experienced spiritual trauma has been hurt in the church (maybe not in a church building or by a specific community but by someone who shares the same faith). What they've experienced is a very real trauma, not a lesser one, with unique pain points that result from deep immersion in and then a sudden split from a spiritual community.

To understand the full impact of that kind of wound, we have to talk about what kind of trauma it actually is. Relational trauma is a category of trauma that's often overlooked or dismissed. It's a kind of trauma that happens when harm is caused within a significant relationship, like with a caregiver, a family member, a partner, or a close friend. While it's harder to identify, the effect this kind of trauma has on the brain and nervous system is the same as any other major trauma. When you're hurt inside a relationship where you expected safety, the damage cuts deeper and lasts longer. Because of how intertwined and complex our relationships within the church are, spiritual communities are often perpetrators of relational trauma.

The saying "The church didn't hurt you—people did!" is an oversimplification that feels dismissive to those who have been wounded inside one. It's the spiritual version of "It's just a flesh wound!" Instead of acknowledging the pain, that mentality trivializes what we've experienced. When someone dismisses our pain, it absolves them of the responsibility to repair it. If they decide it isn't a big deal, that the pain isn't justifiable, then they don't have to sit in the discomfort of acknowledging that something harmful happened. They don't have to look inward at their own heart and behavior, and they don't have to look outward to hold other people accountable to theirs. They don't have to question the system of power that's in place or the motives and integrity of the people who sit in those seats. It's easier to dismiss than to engage. But isn't that what we're called to do?

When we're wounded by a spiritual community, our brain doesn't register it as "Oh, a couple of people hurt my feelings." Our brain registers the event the same way we'd process any other kind of trauma. Parts of our brain shut down. Our nervous system moves into freeze, fight, flight, or fawn, and we sometimes get stuck there. We become reactive, defensive, reclusive, distrusting. We lose weight or gain it. We discover new addictions. We make impulsive, reckless decisions.[2]

I'm sure you can think of times in your life when you've acted like this or, perhaps easier to remember, times when people you know have been reckless in the fallout of pain. I mean, raise your hand if you've ever impulsively reshared a snarky post because it said what you wanted to say about something that happened to you. (Both my hands are up.) Some people, in the processing of their pain, push everyone out, start fights around the dinner table, or are just generally unpleasant to be around. I've done and been all those things. The reason for these responses is simple but incredibly complex: People who have experienced spiritual trauma aren't bitter—they have PTSD.

The church often meets this pain with criticism instead of grace. Instead of having our trauma acknowledged as a deep wound that needs to be cared for, we've been told to get over it, to not get bitter, to forgive, and to move on. As if it could ever be that simple. The church has positioned itself as the voice of correction rather than the hands of healing, and it often condemns the symptoms of trauma without ever addressing the source of that pain.

But this kind of response is not aligned with God's character. God's response to the wounded looks nothing like rejection, insensitivity, or impatience.

- While some spiritual leaders might label hurting people as "troublemakers" or "divisive," God sees and acknowledges our pain. "The Lord is near the brokenhearted; he saves those crushed in spirit" (Psalm 34:18).
- While some leaders value community or religious rules over restoration and healing, Jesus ignores legalistic outrage and heals the hurting (Mark 3:1-6; Matthew 12:9-14; Luke 6:6-11).
- While some communities weaponize Scripture to punish and shame, Jesus sees the whole person, their worth and their humanity, and offers mercy over condemnation (John 8:1-11).
- When broken, sick, and hurting people come into Jesus' presence, he doesn't recoil from them. He welcomes them in, touches them, and makes them whole (Mark 5:25-34; Luke 8:43-48).

- When leaders value their image over relationships, Jesus pulls back a chair and pats the seat, welcoming outsiders to sit at the table (Luke 5:27-32; Matthew 9:10-13).

Repeatedly throughout the life of Christ and the story of God and his people, we see Jesus breaking religious expectations so he can heal, restore, and embrace those the system cast out. God doesn't minimize our wounds. He doesn't shame us for how we process our pain. He doesn't demand that we heal on any sort of timeline or in a way that makes other people comfortable. As you can see in the story of Jesus, he's never really cared about religious comfort. He meets us where we are, exactly as we are.

Jesus never pushed away the questioner, the sinner, or the hurting. He stepped closer to them.

If you've been told that your pain will make you bitter, that your anger makes you a sinner, or that your questions make you unfaithful, remember: Jesus never pushed away the questioner, the sinner, or the hurting. He stepped closer to them. He pulled the hurting and the cast-out into his atmosphere, and he does the same for you.

Two decades after I sat on the living room floor as a little girl and watched my world turn upside down, I sat on my own living room floor and delivered news to Zach that did the same thing to him.

Against all my best efforts and hopes, history repeated itself.

As I relayed what had just happened, I watched Zach go from sitting upright to putting his head in his hands to lying back on the couch, arms spread wide, as if to brace himself from an impact that had already shaken the house down. Eventually, he was on his back on the floor, staring at the ceiling as we spun into an unknown orbit.

Although I'd walked into ministry jaded and expecting betrayal, this still knocked the air out of me. I thought I'd done everything I could to protect myself from feeling this kind of pain again. But here I was, shattered by the church. Again.

When Zach and I were newly married, we were invited to interview for a youth pastor position. We sat in the boardroom and were interviewed by the pastor and a handful of board members. The interview was going well. I was making them laugh, Zach was impressing them with his sincerity and passion for youth ministry. But then I had to go and do the thing I always do—sometimes on purpose but usually on accident—I told the truth. I forgot you're supposed to dress it up and repackage it, especially when you're, I don't know, *interviewing for a job*.

When one of the board members asked me if we had any reservations about accepting the job, all my twenty-two-year-old audacity and complete lack of professionalism and, you know, lack of any common sense at all formed the thought, *Yeah, I do. I don't trust boards.* And then I said those words *out loud*.

To my surprise and yours, we got the job. In fact, they responded to my deeply buried and newly unearthed childhood wound with empathy and compassion. They nodded their heads and said, "Well, we hope to be the board that changes that for you."

And you know what? They did. We were there for four years, and although there were different challenges that led to us leaving a little sooner than we thought we would, it was never the pastor or the board or the people in the church. They treated us well from the interview to our very last day. They loved us well, and we still keep in touch. It was such a blessing to have our first post–college ministry position be such a positive and healing experience.

But in a new church and a new chapter, I was in the fetal position, lost, questioning, angry, and broken in almost every way a person can be broken. Zach and I went into survival mode, pushed everyone out, and became as insular as we could. No input, no output. We needed to heal, and we didn't trust anyone.

When we started trying to assimilate into new churches, my nervous system wasn't ready. Everything familiar was a reminder of what we'd lost. Well, what had been stolen from us. Worship music reminded me of the years Zach and I led worship teams together. That was gone now. Dropping my kids off at Sunday school reminded me of how the leadership sat across from me and told me that no one wanted my three-year-old son in their class. "Turn to your neighbor and say hello" might as well have been, "Look at the people who will slash you to pieces."

My whole body would shake as I walked into the building every Sunday. I flinched at every person's attempt to welcome me in. I side-eyed every invitation and overanalyzed every conversation. I was experiencing what my therapist would later tell me was *hypervigilance*. I was on guard, eyes shifting to every corner of the room, looking for danger, identifying threats, and doing what I needed to do to protect my family.

In the book *Escaping Enemy Mode*, Jim Wilder and Ray Woolridge define *enemy mode* as a brain state that affects the way we view and perceive other people.[3] When we're in enemy mode, we instinctively see other people as threats, operating under the assumption, "You aren't on my side." It makes us hostile and disconnected, and causes us to amplify even the smallest interactions as being bigger and more threatening than they actually are. It turns our relational circuits off so we're unable to befriend or re-friend anymore. When we live in enemy mode, we've adopted an us vs. them mentality, and the longer we're in it, the harder it is to get out.

Enemy mode runs rampant in the Western evangelical church. We learn early on in our faith walk who's "in" and who's "out." Those who don't think like us, believe like us, vote like us, or do church like us are our enemies, whether we call them that or not. For me, growing up in a charismatic denomination, the "them" were Baptists, Catholics, and any belief system that didn't center around the works of the Holy Spirit. Also included were Democrats, people who were divorced, non-Christians in general, and celebrities (unless they made a public declaration of faith and hadn't made any questionable decisions afterward). We prayed for the salvation of all those people, of course—we wouldn't just *judge* them—but they weren't a part of "us."

When you've been hurt in a spiritual community, the reality of "us vs. them" becomes a crushing blow when you become the "them." You know what the people on the inside are thinking and saying about you, because you've thought it and said it too.

When people experience hurt in church, they don't leave in good spirits. They leave broken and bleeding, adrenaline rushing, to get somewhere safe and protect their families from further harm. Enemy mode is instinctually activated inside them, and what comes out often looks like anger or bitterness, but underneath it's usually just fear or pain. The rejection and harm are painful enough in themselves, but what really sends people over the edge isn't usually the event that caused the pain but the lack of nurture and care in the aftermath. Many church communities take on the mentality, "If you aren't a part of *my* church, you aren't a part of *the* church." Not my sheep, not my problem.

Our faith, if it is anything at all, is intrinsically relational. But how can we honor a faith that's communal when we elevate so many other things above community? How do we repair if we value personal peace over unity?

If you like a good Scripture word count like I do, the phrase "one another" is used over one hundred times in ninety-four verses in the New Testament. Many of those verses refer directly to the relationship between brothers and sisters in Christ. They're about loving one another and encouraging us to care for one another in spiritual and practical ways.[4] We're to comfort one another, bring peace to one another, serve one another, accept one another, forgive one another, and try our best not to bite, devour, or consume one another. We're supposed to seek *good* for one another. And I just think that if the people who wrote these letters to the early church and those who canonized them into Scripture and the God who inspired both groups felt that the concept of caring for one another is *that* important, then so should we, you know?

But the reality is that many of us have experienced the opposite of these commands in church spaces. When I reread these verses after Zach and I faced spiritual trauma as adults, I fully scoffed at them. I thought, *Ha! Yeah, right. As if anyone actually does any of those things.* I spent a lot of time looking backward at my painful church experiences and living in the *what-if*s of it all. What if someone—anyone—had stood up for my dad long before he had to stand trial? Maybe it would have never gone that far. What if, instead of being left isolated and alone, we'd been immediately taken in by a community and cared for so we could repair the relational wounds and prevent the trauma from settling into our nervous systems? What if, instead of telling Zach and me to "leave quickly and quietly," the people we reached out to for support told us to not roll over and to report the abuse to an authority? What if someone had spoken up against and to the authoritative powers instead of being privately outraged? What if, instead of blindly following abusive leadership, people had asked curious questions, invited Zach and me to the table, and allowed us to defend ourselves—or, at the very least, speak for ourselves?

How would the trajectory of our lives have changed if things had been handled differently? If we were seen and held instead of cast out, would the experience have been as painful? If people didn't assume, *Well they must have done something wrong,* and instead thought, *It's not my job to determine who deserves my compassion,* would our sense of identity still have been shattered? How would my life and my faith look if the body of Christ had cared more about connection than control? Where would I have been if someone had helped us pick up the pieces of our life instead of watching from a distance, afraid to get too close to our mess?

When we take the "one anothers" of Scripture seriously, they become the principles for how we care for each other. And with these principles, we're equipped not just to care for each other but to be the healers who patch up wounds caused by someone else. We have the power to turn the relational circuits back on in someone's life. Healing other people's hurts is the work of Christ. Some churches focus so much on spreading the gospel and "saving the lost" that they neglect the needs of their immediate spiritual communities. We hinder the spread of the good news when we let those who already believe it be harmed by those who claim to live it. It shouldn't matter if we "agree" with the ferocity of their pain. It isn't our job to figure out who's right and who's wrong. Jesus didn't ask many questions about those he healed. He just healed them.

The Kingdom of God is better when people are healing and healing one another. Do you believe in the mission of Christ so much that you're willing to pick up a cross that isn't yours to carry? When Jesus said that we'd do "even greater things,"[5] I wonder if he saw a future where an entire generation takes responsibility for harm they didn't cause and heals wounds that may not be visible. When Jesus healed, he did it supernaturally, usually instantaneously. The miracles he performed could be seen, touched, and measured—water to wine, storms calmed with a word, a few loaves and fishes multiplied to feed thousands of people. Maybe the "greater things" he said we'd do aren't necessarily in the awe and wonder of instant, tangible healings. What if the miracles we're to perform are the slower, less obvious work of healing the spiritually sick, wounded, traumatized, and broken? What if the bride of Christ can present itself as holy because we have carried one another into wholeness?

The reality is that wounds in a spiritual community slice deep and cause unthinkable harm—harm that often stretches across generations. These wounds cut into our core need as humans to be known and loved and safe. It unhinges fundamental wiring in our brains. What starts as "We don't know who our friends are" becomes "I have no friends," which becomes "I *can't* have friends," which leads to "I'm safer without friends." We're naturally driven to self-preservation, and losing community in a brutal way is a justifiable reason to stay away from that kind of environment indefinitely.

But sometimes someone turns the light back on. Sometimes the wound heals and the wounded person becomes a healer. A church made up entirely of healers isn't some utopian ideal; it's what it was supposed to be in the first place. What if our spiritual wounds were never given the opportunity to fester and spread infection?

I was a walking open wound for a long time—from a little girl on my parents' living room floor to a thirtysomething-year-old wife and mother just trying to survive. The circuits were down, and I liked them that way. But then something started to change.

After we left our church, I was a shell of a person, which is putting it lightly. Zach and I began to unravel our theology of church, and as we did, we couldn't escape the "one anothers." And I did try. Repeatedly. But eventually we both realized that regardless of how long we'd been part of the church, we'd never been a part of one that embodied those commands. Not in the way Scripture requires, anyway. And honestly, I didn't want to be a part of something like that. It was too much. Too close. Too intimate. Too known.

As someone with chronic church pain, I was resistant to the idea that I needed to step *closer*. But as I read the words on the pages of the Bible I was trying not to resent anymore, I couldn't escape the intimacy it described. I wasn't sure if I'd known *anyone* in that way. I didn't know if I was capable of it. It certainly didn't feel safe. But I accepted that if God created me for community, and if he intended his church to be what Paul described in those letters, then I had to be open to relationship. I had to open myself up and let others know me.

And then it all happened—fast and against my will. One day there was a message from Melissa, a woman I used to go to church with. We hadn't gotten to know each other much at church, and we'd both since left, but she wanted to be friends. She remembered a wildly inappropriate joke I'd made about Smurfs in our small group, and I guess that's what made her think I'd make a safe friend. I had edge. She had grit. Maybe we had more in common.

So we got crepes, and she let me know that we were friends now. She gave me ample warning that her friendships weren't fluffy. "I get intense really fast, so hope you're good with that." I wasn't sure I had a choice! To be honest, I didn't want a friendship like that, but I knew I needed it. So I let her in.

Melissa's invitation to friendship was the first of several in a short span of time. Against my best efforts to keep to myself, a few women pushed through the walls and elbowed their way into my life. And I'm grateful.

After a lifetime of keeping people at arm's length, you kind of get used to having things that way. But these new friends saw something in me that was worth knowing, and they stepped past my defensive position and drew me out. By wanting to know me, they made me knowable. They welcomed me, accepted me, and celebrated me.

This was the first time I'd had friends outside the denomination I'd grown up in. It was the first time I had friends who didn't believe the same things I did. It was the first time I didn't need to be theologically vetted before I was allowed a seat at the table. They just pulled out a chair and told me to sit. There were no pretenses, no side-eyes, no demands made of me. Just people who enjoyed my company and wanted to get to know me. It healed me, piece by piece, bit by bit. Some of them stayed in my life, but other relationships have been like waves hitting the shore. Sometimes people crash into your life and fade away, with no ill will or dramatic breakaway—just the natural movements of the relational ocean. But sometimes someone sticks.

Kasey is my stickiest friend. Our friendship story is long and funny and a little dramatic at times, but the most important plot point is that she was one of the first people who turned my relational lights back on after our church ripped me apart. She was kind, empathetic, and generous, and she somehow lived her life without the slightest bit of judgment against anyone.

She listened to my stories, affirmed my pain, drew things out of me that I didn't know were there, and called out things that needed to be called out. She was loving and honest but never told the truth with malice. She taught me how to resolve conflict without burning a bridge and made me believe I was worth knowing. She said things to me that no one had ever said before, like "Your needs are not a problem" and "You're not bothering me by existing" and "No, I will not delete your number just because we had a fight." She taught me how to trust—not just because she could be trusted, but by being a good friend to me even when I tried to shut her out. She kept her light on for me. She healed a heart she didn't break and taught me how to do the same.

Relationships are complicated things, even without spiritual and relational trauma. But when your relationships are interwoven with your spiritual identity, the loss of one often means the loss of the other. When a spiritual community rejects a member or pushes them out or ices them out or edges them to the outskirts of their circle, it causes damage that can't be fixed easily. It fractures an intrinsic part of a person's identity, and that fracture affects their ability to connect, to attach, and consequently, to heal. But when you find someone who turns the light on for you, those relational circuits in your brain start to flicker again . . . a little bit at a time.

I once saw a tweet from Jackie Hill Perry that said, "Know what healed my church hurt? The church." At the time, I wanted to throw my phone across the room. It felt trite, dismissive—like someone telling me to just get over it. The church had rejected me, wounded me, cast me out. Now it was supposed to heal me? Hard pass.

My frustration wasn't about her words—it was more about my understanding of the church at the time. To me, church was a single institution, a system that had failed me aggressively and repeatedly. My only understanding of the church was my limited experience with it. I'd been in the same denomination since I was born. My parents, siblings, cousins, and grandparents on both sides of my family had all been in that denomination. I didn't have friends outside my belief framework or outside my denominational circle—a denomination that I'd now decided to leave and separate myself from entirely. If that was what church was, I didn't want it. If that's where I was supposed to heal, I'd stay sick.

The thing about the church is that before it's a denomination or a building or a group of people, it's a living, breathing organism. It isn't contained by structures and systems; it's an extension of Jesus himself. People who are in Christ live and move and breathe by him and through him, and they follow where he leads. And like any good Shepherd, he leads them to good pastures. After we left the church, the Shepherd led his flock to me, and they didn't look like any flock I'd ever seen. They weren't tied to the same church, the same denomination, or even the same belief systems. They simply were led by Jesus, loved Jesus, and saw in me what *he* saw in me: a sheep with a couple of broken legs who needed a Shepherd and a flock to care for her.

As it turned out, Jackie was right. The church *did* heal my church hurt, but if I'm being honest, that's putting it lightly. They didn't just heal something that happened to me that they had nothing to do with; they took responsibility for every hurt I'd experienced, every lie I'd believed, every belief I'd doubted, and they showed me what it means to be a part of the family of God. They made eye contact with my pain and weren't afraid of it. They listened to my doubts and didn't panic about them. They didn't wait for me to "get past" my mental health issues before they invited me to the table. They didn't wait until I was certain of what I believed to recognize the value of my presence and influence. They called out the good in me, challenged the weaknesses in me, and taught me what it means to be safe in Christ.

This didn't happen in a singular group in a singular place. These were individuals, with no connections to each other, who showed up in my life in the most unexpected places. They didn't know they were healing me. They were just moving in Christ. They didn't ask for recognition for the good things they did for me; they just did them. And they didn't do them because Jesus told them to; they did it because that's who he compelled them to *be*. It was never about me but about who they were in Christ. With these people being the extension of his presence on earth, I learned to trust again. They healed thirty-year-old Kristen . . . and they healed nine-year-old Kristen too.

If you've been fractured in a relationship with someone who shared the same faith as you, the idea that you will ever trust someone in a similar space again may sound impossible—maybe even a little offensive. If you were a part of a church that called itself a family, only to have them push you out or abandon you, or if you've ever been iced out because of your doubts and questions, you might think it's safer to be alone. If you experienced a crisis so heavy and complex that people were too scared or overwhelmed to step into it with you, or if you simply grew and changed, and that change was seen as a threat, you might feel like community will never be worth the risk, ever again. And that's valid. Betrayal, rejection, and harm in spiritual communities will always carry a specific kind of sting. But it won't always take you all the way out. When those broken parts of your identity heal, you don't see people as a threat anymore. You learn to let people in and start to trust again. Eventually, you get to the point where you're secure enough in who you are—in your worth, your purpose, your place in the Kingdom of God—that the hurts that come your way can become a part of your story, but not the entire book.

When our identity in Christ is secure and our sense of self has a strong, rooted foundation, relationships can be a *joy*. I've found that they are ultimately worth the risk.

When you find someone who turns those relational circuits back on, someone who feels safe, someone who loves you and welcomes you for who you are and what you're wrestling with, lean in. Take your time. You can inch your way back into relationships if that's what you need to do—so long as you keep moving. For most of my life, I didn't know who my friends were. For years—decades, even—I didn't care to have friends at all. But now I know who my friends are.

You might not know who your friends are today. But you will.

2

The Pressure-Driven Life

The Cost of Spiritual Perfection

CRACKER BARREL, MIDDLE TENNESSEE, 1998

I'M SITTING IN A CRACKER BARREL with my basketball team. I'm twelve years old, and we've just lost our first away game. Not that you'd know that by looking at us. We're having a blast—no one cares that we lost. I didn't even get to play. I don't care about that either. I'm just happy to be at the table. The girls on the team are all older than me, better basketball players than me, and so effortlessly cool.

The conversation turns to all the "bad" things they've done. I can't believe what I'm hearing. They're so cool. I need to make them think I'm cool too, so I lie and tell them I do that stuff too. They don't buy it.

"Yeah, right, Kristen. Your dad's a pastor. You're a goody-two-shoes." They laugh. I don't know what a *goody-two-shoes* is, but I know I don't want to be one.

I feel something stirring in my chest for the first time. I need to prove myself. I need to be bad. I know what I'm going to do.

As we finish our dinner, I reach toward the middle of the table and pick up the triangle game that is standard at Cracker Barrel tables. "I'm gonna steal this," I whisper.

Their mouths open wide. This is exactly the reaction I was hoping for. I smirk and put the game on my lap.

My heart is racing as we stand up to leave. I slide the game under my shirt. Our waitress follows us to the door and opens it for us. She smiles and says, "Good night," and as she does, she looks at my shirt. Her eyebrows furrow.

Shoot, I think. *I'm caught.* But she doesn't say anything, and I make it to the school van. I pull out the game and look at my teammates.

They chuckle and someone yells, "Hey, Coach! Kristen just stole something from Cracker Barrel!"

I don't know what I was expecting from this, but I definitely was not expecting to get ratted out so fast. *I thought we were in this together! I thought we were bonding!* My heart is going to burst through the walls of my chest. I'm definitely getting arrested. Kicked out of school. I went too far. I didn't just do something bad; I COMMITTED A CRIME.

I get home and bury the game at the bottom of the trash can. Destroy the evidence. If Coach tells Mom and Dad, I'll tell them I was just kidding. I lied to make the girls think I was cool, but I didn't actually steal anything! After my parents go to bed, I dig through my mom's purse and find a couple of dollars. I stuff the money inside an envelope and look up the Cracker Barrel address in the phone book. I write a letter and say I'm sorry.

"Dear Who It May Concern," I write. "I accidentally stole this game from one of your stores tonight. I'm not going to say which one, but I'm sorry. I hope this is enough. Please don't arrest me."

I don't sign my name, and I stay up all night praying for forgiveness. I'll make this up to God too. I beg him not to send me to hell . . . or jail.

I had a happy childhood. It's easy to reframe our childhood through the pain we process later. Without meaning to, we can reshape our memories, emphasizing things that didn't feel quite as big back then or filling in the blanks with the hurt we feel now.

My story is complicated, as most stories are. There was pain in my childhood, but joy and goodness were there too. Not every wound comes from a dramatic fall. Just like infections can grow in our bodies unnoticed for a time, spiritual malformation is the quiet shaping of our souls in ways that distort the image of God, ourselves, and what it means to be loved. That malformation doesn't always happen in obvious ways—it can happen quietly, beneath every good intention.

My childhood? Well. My childhood smelled like vanilla, varnished wood, and the faint dust of church carpet.

I grew up running laps between the pews of sanctuaries with my brothers on Saturday afternoons and sitting in them as still and quiet as I could on Sunday mornings. I replaced air fresheners (the jelly ones that wiggled when you poked them) while my mom flipped through the church's huge box of transparencies.* I walked up and down the pews, picking up hymnals and Bibles

* I feel truly archaic saying this, but before the digital age, we projected the words to songs on clear plastic sheets called *transparencies*.

and putting them back in their wooden slots on the back of the pews. My brothers and I would gather all the communion cups and throw them in the trash while Dad did whatever pastors do in their offices during the week.

When we weren't helping my parents with something, we played hide-and-seek in the sanctuary, did homework in empty Sunday school classrooms, ate McDonald's at the boardroom desk in my dad's office before Wednesday-night service, or told ghost stories in the dark balcony of the sanctuary. When I say, "I grew up in the church," what I mean is that I *literally* grew up inside churches. I didn't "go" to church. I lived there. And when I say, "I lived there," I don't mean I was there a lot; I mean I *actually* lived in them. Two of them. They were our legal address. I slept next to a copy machine.

Church wasn't so much what we did or where we went, but who we were. That extended into my larger family, as all my parents' siblings were pastors, missionaries, and ministry leaders. The conversations at Christmas and Thanksgiving were stories of miracles, debates over theological ideas, church drama for *days*, and attendance reports that were more big fish tales for fishers of men than verifiable facts. Our conversations were often broken up by any one of the women in my family sitting at the piano (which could be found in the living room of all their houses) and leading us in a hymn or chorus. You could ask them to play anything your heart wanted to hear, and they'd be able to play it, right off the top of their heads, as if worship was their second language. Every singer in the room (which was pretty much everybody) would slip into harmony, and their voices would blend in a way that only families' voices can, and it was beautiful, safe, and fun.

And although there have been times when I've resented (and

recontextualized) the world I grew up in, time gives perspective and fills in the hurts with grace, nuance, and more understanding. All in all, I was fortunate to be raised by and around people who wanted to be good. Faith was a priority and a nonnegotiable, but it wasn't high control or abusive. We were just really, *really* Christian. As I heard Nate Bargatze say once, "My parents were '90s Christians. So . . . they were the *most* Christian."

By the time the grandchildren (the third generation of Pentecostal Christians) were growing up and going to college, we joked that ministry was the family business. Several of us picked up the mantle of our fathers and mothers and went to Bible college, married pastors and worship leaders, and dedicated our lives to Christian service. Even though I knew I had other options as far as careers went, I never really considered them. Ministry was all I knew. It was all I'd *ever* known. The same was true for my dad, whose dad was a pastor, and for my mom, whose dad was also a pastor. This was their world, and it was mine as well. And with that world came expectations—spoken and unspoken.

My entire life was just . . . Jesus. We never lived close to family, so my family was my dad's flock. My life revolved, at every moment, around the churches he was pastoring. These were the people we considered when we made decisions about where we went, what we did, and how we dressed. It was the framework that built my beliefs, my worldviews, my paradigms, and my entire identity. I was born into the church, and it became as intricately woven into my DNA as any other part of me.

Like many pastors' kids, I felt my identity didn't belong to me as much as it belonged to the family business. While my parents never overtly projected expectations onto my siblings and me because of my dad's position in the church, the culture we were in demanded it. Every move I made reflected on the pastors in my life. Every good decision or impressive accomplishment was accredited to their influence (whether real or assumed). Every questionable decision was pointed back to them: "What would your dad think?" Or the soul-crushing "Your grandfather would be so disappointed in you."

We were interconnected, my pastors and me, and we always will be. As an adult, I've come to a sort of peace with the imprints of the legacies that came before me. As a kid, I was genuinely confused by what my dad's job had to do with *me*.

Oh, but it had *everything* to do with me.

Most kids have identifiers other than their parents' jobs. My brothers had sports and good grades and instruments. I didn't have any of that. I wasn't particularly talented at anything other than the relatively solitary craft of writing. In reality, we moved around too often for me to be known for anything other than what my family came into town to do. I wanted to be known for being myself, not being Chuck's daughter or Chris's sister or Brother Jordan's granddaughter. My identity was so wrapped up in everyone else that I worked overtime to establish myself apart from everyone else.

Every time we moved, I picked a new personality. When we lived in Tennessee, I quickly junked my New Jersey accent and adopted a thick Southern drawl. When my only friends were into punk music, I retired my Britney Spears and Rachael Lampa CDs and got into New Found Glory and Simple Plan. (CDs I would later cut into pieces as a dramatic purge of secular influence. As one did in the early 2000s.) I changed my name, made up nicknames, went out with guys I didn't like that much just to see what it was like. I chopped off all my hair. I wore bracelets up to my elbows. I wore sweater-vests over button-downs. I became hyper-charismatic. I became a bit of a stoic. I acted like I didn't care what people thought of me while actively trying harder than anyone has ever tried to get people to like me.

I was exhausting. (And I was exhausted.)

I just wanted to be anyone other than *just* a pastor's kid. I resented it. But that's who I was. And I wasn't a very good one. If you aren't a pastor's kid, I bet you have an image in your head of what they're like. Most people picture one of two types. There's the kid who knows every Bible verse and is a leader at home, at church, and at school—a shining example to all the other Christian kids. Or there's the Jessica Lovejoy type—rebellious, manipulative, with a nose piercing and a secret tattoo.

There's no middle ground, of course. Every pastor's kid is either a golden child or a train wreck.

Although I did serve a bit of time in Junior Bible Quiz and was a ribbon-holding member, I also secretly got my belly button pierced on the Jersey Shore when I was sixteen by asking a stranger to pretend to be my mom and sign the consent form for me. I taught Sunday school and led worship, but I also flipped my mom off behind her back. I was *complicated*, okay? I was never mistaken for the perfect pastor's kid, and I wasn't Jessica Lovejoy either, although I was much more likely to be identified as the latter than the former.

To be honest, I preferred it that way. It's easier to be slightly above a low bar than to reach for a bar you couldn't possibly grab anyway. I fully accepted that I was the black sheep of the family. I was the one who didn't exhibit "good" behavior naturally, so I was the bad one.

It wasn't that I wanted to be. I wanted to be good and to be seen as good. I wanted to please God and my parents. I wanted to be chosen for ministry opportunities and for people to say that I'd do great and powerful things for God. But because my personality was a bit more . . . precocious, if you will, those labels weren't given to me freely. I wasn't a serious person. I was goofy and clumsy and made impulsive decisions. I wasn't the mini adult that a lot of pastors' kids are. I was just a kid living my life, trying to get away with things I knew I shouldn't have been doing.

To a lot of people in my world, I was just a sinner. A big, bad, rebellious, probably hell-bound sinner. Except I wasn't. I just sort of accepted that story. I wasn't actually bad. But I *felt* bad. I earnestly wanted to follow Jesus. There wasn't a single day of my childhood, my adolescence, or my early adulthood that I wanted to rebel against God. Not one. I loved him. I wanted him to love me. And I was *way* too afraid of hell to attempt to sin beyond the scope of what I thought was relatively forgivable.

If you don't count my brief detour into petty theft of restaurant triangle games, I was a good kid. My love for God was genuine. And it frustrated and confused me when the choices I made were spiritualized into a battle for my soul. I'd given my soul to Jesus. Why did it feel like I wasn't getting anything right? Why did it feel like every decision I made had spiritual weight? There were so many voices preaching about holiness and being right before God, but I didn't know what that meant. All I knew was that the devil was after my soul and that every choice was either fleeing from temptation or giving him a foothold. I didn't know there was a balance to be found. I also didn't have a clue what a foothold was.

I felt the tension between who I saw myself to be (a selfish, broken, bad person), who I wanted to be (a good, holy, loved, and likable person), and who God wanted me to be (a perfect, sinless person). The bar was unreachable and unrealistic, and I hated myself because of it. I was pretty sure God hated me too.

Every night I prayed that God would make me a better person. I begged him to change the way I was wired—to make me more like my cousins and my older brother and the other teenagers who never got into trouble the way I did. I felt the weight of even the tiniest infraction in my heart and lived every moment flinching, waiting for the blow from heaven that would take me out.

The blow never came, because that's not who God is, but I didn't know that yet. I thought grace had to be earned, and if that was the case, there was no earning for me. Yet even as I felt defeated and unloved and unwanted by God, I wanted to please him. I wanted to be a good girl. I thought I wasn't good enough to reach the bar. I had no idea the problem wasn't me; it was the bar.

A faith that's centered on behavior is difficult for people who struggle with behavior. Maybe you've spent years trying to figure out why you can't seem to get it right when it comes to spiritual things. You compare yourself to other people and wonder why they don't seem to struggle with . . . *anything*. They make friends easily. They're elevated to positions of leadership. People respect them, they always get an invitation to the table, and faith seems so simple for them. Meanwhile, you carry shame about self-control seeming out of reach, about not remembering all the social rules and cues, about prayers and promises that never work for you the way they do for other people. Maybe you hate the parts of yourself that feel broken that you didn't choose.

I know that feeling well.

Now that I'm an adult, a mother, and someone who has spent a few years collecting diagnoses like Pokémon ("Gotta catch 'em all!" And I have!), I'm able to see with more clarity. As I grew and learned more about myself, I realized that many of the things I struggled with weren't moral or spiritual failings, but simply differences in the way my mind worked. The bar I thought I needed to reach to receive God's goodness was a bar I was *never* going to reach. Not because I was committed to a life of sin and rebellion, but because my brain just wasn't wired the way others expected it to be or the way I wanted it to be.

If no one has ever told you that the way your brain works is not a spiritual failure, let me be the first. It's not. It's just part of who you are. What might look like sin to other people is probably just survival. I certainly didn't know that. Neither did the people around me. Christian kids in the '90s didn't get diagnosed with anything other than "original sin." We weren't neurodivergent, we were neuro-disobedient! So, of course, I felt like there was something spiritually wrong with me.

In many faith frameworks, we're taught that a life surrendered to Christ is evidenced by works, which is translated to behavior, so we scale the integrity of a person's commitment to Christ by the choices they make. And you know what? Okay. Sure. That's fair. But sometimes people do and say all the right things and their hearts are dark. Even the most well-behaved person is capable of evil and harm. And sometimes the most genuine followers of Christ do things that make you scratch your head and go, *Huh?*

It's almost as if we look at the outside and God looks at the heart, eh?

If behavior can't be the universal measuring stick for a life surrendered to Christ, then perhaps a bit more nuance and flex are needed in the framework. As children, we seek validation and acceptance from our families. As adults, we seek the same thing from our peers and spiritual authorities. We want to be accepted and feel like we belong, and when it feels like our belonging is hinged on parts of us we can't control, we may feel defeated, worthless, hopeless, rejected, and alone.

There are so many potential reasons for someone to exhibit behavior that doesn't align with a community's expectation of a follower of Christ. Abuse, trauma, disability, mental health struggles, developmental delay, even cultural differences can cause someone to act in a way that some communities interpret as sin. But all those things, while not single identifiers of a person, are undeniably part of who we are. How do we honor the image of God in every person, regardless of what we assume about them based on their choices and behaviors?

If we want to honor the image of God in others, we have to start by first understanding how that image gets shaped and distorted in ourselves. Our families of origin determine a lot about how we develop, how we attach, what we think of the world, what we believe about God, and how we view ourselves. But they aren't the only factors. Our personalities and the way we're wired determine way more than we realize. It's why we might have totally different experiences from our siblings despite being raised in the same house, by the same people, at the same time. It doesn't mean that one person is telling the truth and the other is lying; it just means that different people experience the same things in different ways. I am the second born of five kids, and I can tell you with certainty that my experience as the eldest daughter is wildly different from my sister's, who was born eight and a half years after me. That's not just because my parents and our circumstances were different; it's also because we're different people and we process and experience things in different ways.

As a kid, I internalized my experiences and operated in extremes. Everything was all or nothing, black or white. I needed clarity and rules that made sense. I was such a literal, binary thinker that my parents nicknamed me Amelia Bedelia. You know, like the storybook maid who thought "dressing the turkey" meant putting clothes on it? That was me. Nuance didn't stand a chance. When I decided to *really* follow Jesus, not because I was born into faith but because I wanted to, I went all in. Hardcore, certified Jesus freak. I still have the piece of notebook paper where I wrote the goals for my life at age fifteen. At the top of the list, I wrote: "Lead 5 people to Christ by age 16."* In my *Chicken Soup for the Teenage Soul* journal, I answered the prompt "Write about your dreams. It'll be fun to look back 10 years from now and see how many dreams came true." Sold-out-for-Jesus Kristen wrote,

> Well, if I read this ten years from now, my dream hasn't come true yet. I want to die for Christ. He died for me, it's the least I can do to repay that debt. What better way than to die? . . . My dream sounds really bad. "I dream to die." But that's exactly what I want! To die! Why would I want to stay here in this sin-infested world?

Oof, right? Someone get that girl some new dreams—that is *bleak*. And the wild thing is that no one ever sat me down and systematically taught me that a good Christian wants to die a

* I didn't. I gave up on that when I discovered boys.

martyr's death, but I absorbed this message nonetheless. My brain is wired to do the most, so of course I was drawn to the most extreme way to be a devoted follower of Christ. Sure, going to church and being a good Christian are great, but *have you tried being martyred?*

Outside of daydreaming about the ways I could die and the words that would be written about my prolific life afterward, I didn't know much else about following Jesus. I read books, I listened to Christian music, I had some Christian friends, I went to church every Sunday morning and Sunday night and Wednesday night and occasionally on the weekend, if there was something going on. I was eager to prove myself as a committed Christian, but outside of being killed for it, I didn't know what else to do.

In the churches I grew up in, and in my "'90s Christian is the most Christian" family of pastors and preachers and missionaries, people were celebrated for their spiritual commitment and fortitude. Baptisms were as big a deal as birthdays. Aunts and uncles cut checks for nieces and nephews going on mission trips. Fathers swelled with pride when telling their peers and congregants about the work their children were doing for the Lord. I didn't recognize it at the time, but my self-worth was largely sourced in how my faith was perceived and applauded by the people I loved and respected. I was looking for attention and validation, but I wasn't exactly sure what steps were required to get it. I misinterpreted the praise other people received for their good works as proof of acceptance and value.

I felt unseen and misunderstood, and I interpreted the world in a really simple way: If I make good choices, I'm loved. If I make bad choices, I'm hated. My brain was wired to see things as being one thing or the other. I thought I could only be good and loved or bad and hated. My identity hinged on being accepted, and I believed that acceptance hinged on being a good Christian.

It was in the quiet of my room, not at an altar or at an emotionally charged youth rally, at fifteen years old, that I decided to leave my life of debauchery (ha!) behind. I said the sinner's recommitment prayer (the prayer you pray when you're already a Christian but you're not sure if you're still saved, so you top yourself off with another one), and I wrote letters to my parents asking them to forgive me for the ways I'd wronged them and announced that I was committed to following Jesus.

That same week, I cut off all my hair. We were on spring break, and I wanted to go back to school a changed woman. To me, that meant chopping my hair, because my hair had sin in it and I wanted it gone. If that doesn't make any sense to you, congrats! You're not a victim of Y2K Christian youth culture.

When I returned to our small Christian school after break, everything felt different. I was happy and excited. I felt different. The air around me felt different. I *so* wanted someone to notice, but I'd gotten so used to being seen one way that I didn't have much hope of being seen any differently.

I felt like a screw-up and thought I'd always be seen as one. I'd strayed too far. I'd sinned too much. It was my fault no one could see how I'd changed. I grew tired of waiting for someone to tell me they were proud of the work I was doing. I knew it wasn't right for me to serve Jesus so others would see me, but I still wanted them to.

And then someone noticed: one of my teachers, Mr. Bill Matko. I didn't know he'd been paying attention, but good teachers always do. He pulled me aside in the hallway one day and said, "Okay, talk to me. What's going on? You're different." His face lit up as I told him about how I'd decided to really follow Jesus and what I was doing to honor God.

As I talked, he smiled and his eyes watered, and he pulled me into a big hug and told me he was proud of me and that he couldn't wait to see what Jesus did with my life. It was a simple moment—quick, fleeting. I'm not sure we ever had a private conversation again after that. But I felt seen. He saw my earnestness, and he believed me.

I was a little girl on an island, with little direction, and he wrapped me up in a hug and told me he was proud of me. It felt like a tangible expression of the tender love of a heavenly Father. It was the first time I felt like someone was seeing me for who I was becoming, not just the mistakes I'd made. Mr. Matko didn't have a preconceived narrative about my story or low expectations for me. He just saw me. I felt from him what Jesus felt toward me, and I held on for dear life.

With that interaction, I gained the confidence to pick up some new identifiers. I wasn't *just* a pastor's kid. I wasn't *just* good or bad. I was a good person who loved Jesus and also made mistakes. It wasn't an overnight transformation, but that was the start of a new seed of my identity. It sparked a curiosity in me to discover more about who I was in Jesus, apart from the identity I was born into or the narratives I believed about myself.

There's a term for this, of course. It's called *differentiation*. It's the pivotal process when we mature past the point of identifying solely with our family of origin and begin to see ourselves as individuals—as part of a unit but not the unit alone. That separation is painful and uncomfortable. If you're the one differentiating, there's grief in no longer seeing your parents and family as infallible. If you're the one being differentiated from, there's sadness in what feels like rejection. How can you *not* take it personally? You pour the entirety of who you are—your faith, your jokes, your whole *DNA*—into another human, and they have the audacity to say they want to be different from you?

But how can a person stay the same? The parent and the child let go of each other and begin the awkward dance of existing in parallel lines, no longer on the same one.

Childhood provides the foundation for who we become and how we see and understand ourselves, but identity is something that's continuously shaped, long past when we separate our identity from our families. There are parts of us that are genetically and divinely woven in, but there are so many other parts that are the product of the environment and influences around us. Which is to say, the way we were isn't the way we'll always be—for better or worse.

When we choose to follow Jesus, whether as a child or as an adult, our beliefs look a lot like the environment our faith is nurtured in. As our faith integrates with our identity, we see ourselves through the lens of that framework. For example, if your faith was born in an environment that teaches that women should be mothers and wives and homemakers, you might start to feel like your identity as a believer hinges on whether you can become those things and whether you can do them well. If your faith was shaped in a belief system that taught that speaking in tongues is a requirement for all believers, you might question whether you're truly a Christian if you can't speak in tongues. If you're taught that having depression or anxiety means you don't have enough faith, your struggles with those issues might cause you to feel like you're broken in some way, because if you were a strong enough Christian, you wouldn't struggle. If your church community teaches that Christians shouldn't have close relationships with non-Christians, you might feel like you have to cut ties with your parents, siblings, or close friends who don't share your beliefs.

But what if you don't get married? What if you don't (or can't) have children? What if you have physical, mental, or emotional limitations that affect your ability to perform tasks the way your environment expects you to? What if you're a single mom and you can't homeschool your children or stay home with them? What if you have a chemical imbalance or trauma that causes you to struggle with depression and anxiety? What if you don't speak in tongues? What if you come from a family that loves you deeply and is good to you but doesn't believe the same things you do? What if your identity and the way you're wired as a human being doesn't align with what your belief framework demands of you? What happens when something that is taught to be the "right" identity is something you, personally, cannot grasp?

I can tell you what happens. You stop seeing yourself clearly.

Instead of seeing yourself the way God sees you, you can only see your perceived failures, whether those are simply part of who you are or things you've chosen. And because you can't see yourself clearly, you can't see your strengths, your gifts, and the ways you're an asset to the people around you and the communities you're in. You only see the ways you don't measure up. It's differentiation's evil twin, because it leads to being ostracized. Shame throws a dark, ugly filter over everything that makes you who you are.

Shame causes us to stop seeing God clearly. It fractures the image of God in us in ways that are not irreparable but often require a complex healing process and a generous time frame. When your faith framework and faith community demand absolute compliance, without generosity or nuance, those who can't comply, for whatever reason, are left feeling rejected, broken, and worthless. Being abandoned and rejected by our spiritual family is often a catalyst for the belief that God has abandoned and rejected us as well. We torture ourselves trying to change things about us that can't (or shouldn't) be changed, and when those things remain unchanged, we either give up and walk away, dejected and angry, or we lie.

How often do we reshape ourselves into something untrue because we hate who we are and we want to be who we think God wants us to be (or who our church families expect us to be)? We hear a theology of holiness, and a malformation takes root, causing us to believe that God withholds his love and goodness until we meet his expectations of perfection. That malformation makes us hate who we are. Our walk with Christ becomes about doing rather than being.

Instead of accepting his love and being formed by his grace, we try to perform well enough for him to love us and for our spiritual communities to accept us. When we feel that we're at risk of being abandoned or hated or misunderstood, we hide the parts of ourselves we don't feel safe exposing. But hiding fractures us. We can only hide for so long before we start to crack and eventually break—often harming the people around us as well. When people see what we've been hiding, they might feel confused and hurt, maybe even disappointed. They might feel sad that we didn't feel safe showing them who we are. Or they might be angry that we pretended to be something we aren't.

And perhaps most of all, not telling the truth about ourselves hurts *us*. When we write a narrative about ourselves that isn't true, it's a form of self-harm. No matter the motivation, it turns into self-hatred and causes significant damage.

We betray ourselves when we

- pretend we don't struggle with the things we struggle with
- view ourselves as irredeemably broken
- downplay our accomplishments out of "humility"
- exaggerate our flaws
- accept undeserved correction or discipline, even when it comes from abusive authority
- hide or lie about the things we like, read, listen to, or watch because we're afraid we'll be judged for them
- chronically hide what we feel, think, or believe out of fear or self-preservation

Sometimes we hide to survive, and that may be the wise thing to do for a season. But we can't stay in hiding. We can only live fractured for so long. To live fully in Christ and to see Christ fully, we have to see ourselves clearly and live honestly. Even the parts of our hearts and lives that need changing aren't meant to stay hidden. We can't change what we keep in the dark, and we can't live abundantly when we're in hiding.

At the root of every lie we tell about ourselves or every part of ourselves we feel we need to hide is the belief that we aren't safe in Christ. We aren't confident in who we are because we aren't sure if Christ accepts who we are. Or we're *sure* that he doesn't accept us. So we deny the parts of ourselves that we think will cost us our approval in his Kingdom and with his people.

My transition to motherhood was a rough one. At twenty-four years old, I didn't know enough about myself or motherhood to know that it wasn't going to be a seamless transition. I didn't know what postpartum depression was. I didn't know what anxiety was. I didn't know that my stomach wouldn't disappear the moment I delivered my baby. I didn't know that breastfeeding would hurt. I didn't know that I could be so tired, lonely, and sad. The only examples of motherhood I'd had up to that point were women who seemed to love it and thrive in it. I did not. I was *miserable.*

I hated every second of being pregnant. I threw up the whole time. I didn't live near family and had no close friends to help me during those first few years of motherhood, so I just wallowed. Then I had another baby, and by the time the third one came, I was a fraction of the person I'd been before. I started having panic attacks, night terrors, disassociation, and sleep paralysis. I had no friends, no groups, no support. I kept everything I was feeling bottled inside for one simple reason: I thought it was my fault.

When you internalize the belief that the core of who you are is inescapably *bad*, that becomes the framework for every shortcoming or struggle you have. When you believe every problem has a spiritual solution, you only have yourself to blame when things don't go as you prayed they would. If you believe every problem in your life can be traced back to a spiritual cause, it leaves little room for practical solutions or leaning on your community or seeking answers outside your own spiritual strength. When your most dominant identifier is *broken*, it's difficult for joy and peace to cohabitate in your heart.

Having small children meant I could no longer serve in full-time ministry with Zach. Being on a small salary meant we only had one car that I didn't have access to because he used it to go to work. Not being able to work or do ministry or go anywhere left me with one job and one identifier: mom.

I wanted to believe that that was my highest calling, so I tried to fully commit myself to it. And I did. But I was suffering. And because I believed my "highest calling" was something I was failing at miserably, I felt like there was nothing about me worth salvaging. Motherhood was all I had, and I wasn't good at it, so I felt worthless. Worthless to my kids, to my husband, to my church, and to God himself.

When we shake hands with the belief that God views us as worthless, we fracture the most crucial part of our identity: that we're loved by our Creator. When we believe that God doesn't value us, we believe the same lie the snake in the garden of Eden told Adam and Eve: that God is against us. If we're reflections of God and we're made in his image, what happens to our sense of self and our sense of belonging when we believe we aren't loved and valued by him?

> When Jesus said, "The truth will set you free," he wasn't talking about a belief system. He was talking about himself.

Often, our entire belief framework falls to pieces. Our sadness turns to anger. Anger turns to resentment. Resentment turns to bitterness. All the things that drew us to Christ become ammo in the battle to prove that God has betrayed us.

Why would God make me in his image just to make me a failure? Why would he give everyone else the ability to be a good mother, to have fully balanced chemicals in their brain, to have the right gifts of the Spirit, to move through life effortlessly and with great spiritual power, just to leave me struggling, fumbling, and never measuring up?

The way we view ourselves becomes the lens through which we see God, and when we feel like we're broken, we blame him for not fixing that brokenness. Self-hatred eventually just becomes hatred. It's a poison that we pass down to our children and that gets projected onto our relationships. We withdraw from good things and indulge in harmful ones because we believe that's what we deserve. We reject intimacy with God, because the closer we get to him, the worse we feel about ourselves. We may go through the motions of faith, but we don't let it internalize and take root because we hate ourselves too much to go any deeper.

When we adopt beliefs without thinking through them critically, scripturally, and in community, those beliefs become rigid, unexamined absolute truths. Absolute truths are great when they're *actually* absolute, but something isn't true unless it's true all the time. It's only when our circumstances, genetic makeup, trauma, or crises collide with those "truths" that we realize things aren't as black and white as we previously believed. If we refuse to invite nuance and grace into our understanding, we end up breaking ourselves apart in the struggle to comply with a belief that's harming us.

God never intended for us to live bound by falsehoods that distort his character or our own. When Jesus said, "The truth will set you free" (John 8:32), he wasn't talking about a belief system. He was talking about himself. When we source our identity in who he actually is rather than our distortions of him, we experience the wholeness he promises.

Wholeness isn't an abstract concept or something that we will only grasp when heaven comes to earth. It's the tangible, lived reality of the Kingdom of God. Isaiah 61 describes the Messiah as the one who binds up the brokenhearted, proclaims freedom for the captives, and frees us from the prison of darkness. He doesn't just expose lies we've believed; he repairs the damage they've done. This is the radical redemption we're invited into: that even in the places where lies have shaped the deepest parts of our identity, the Truth himself sets us free and entirely reforms us.

This is why the solution to identity-shattering "absolute truths" isn't to double down or to reject them entirely but to shift our focus to who Christ is and who he says *we* are. Confidence in who we are in Christ reshapes our identity and dismantles the lies that previously defined us. "If anyone is in Christ, he is a new creation; the old has passed away, and see, the new has come! . . . That is, in Christ, God was reconciling the world to himself, not counting their trespasses against them, and he has committed the message of reconciliation to us" (2 Corinthians 5:17, 19). Our sin isn't held against us. We are reconciled, new—the past is gone. We are deeply loved.

When we trust that we're fully known and fully loved in Christ, deception loses its grip. It's a lot harder for lies to shatter us when the foundation of our lives is God's unchanging, absolute love for us. Healing comes not just from unlearning lies but from anchoring ourselves in what has always been true: that we belong to him and that he is making us whole.

When our confidence in Christ metabolizes into our entire system of thinking and being, it brings confidence in ourselves too. Not in a self-serving, self-focused kind of way, but in the way of children who know they're loved. We can hold our heads higher because we know we were created by a God who believes our head deserves a crown. We speak clearer because we're loved by a God who gave us a voice and is proud when we use it. We love deeper because we know what it means to be loved. We give more freely because we know that our Father will never leave us lacking.

We learn to let go of the things that don't matter and hold tight to the things that do. We no longer identify ourselves by who we used to be or the traumas we've experienced or the narratives that other people have written about us. Instead, we embrace what God has said about us, and we walk confidently in that truth. We learn that we can't hate ourselves into righteousness and we can't earn our way into the good graces of our heavenly Father. It's ours by birthright.

> You can't earn your way into the good graces of your heavenly Father. It's yours by birthright.

God doesn't identify us the way we identify ourselves or the way other people have identified us. He doesn't shame us as sinners or failures, and he isn't shaking his head in disappointment at us. He calls us beloved.

- He delights in us (Zephaniah 3:17).
- He defines us by who we are now, not who we once were (2 Corinthians 5:17).
- He sees us as redeemed, chosen, and deeply loved (Ephesians 1:4-5).
- He hasn't rejected or abandoned us (Deuteronomy 31:8; Joshua 1:9).

There are no caveats to his love. He just does. He's with you. He enjoys you. Let the truth of those words sink into your bones, and let yourself be redefined by them.

3

Dare You to Doubt

When Your Belief Breaks the Rules

THE CHURCH THAT BROKE ME

I'M SITTING ACROSS FROM HIM, our knees almost touching. He's taller than me, but that isn't the only thing that makes me feel small. He's the kind of guy who stares at you and doesn't say anything, even as you try to fill the awkward space with words. His eyes are wide, fixed, and unblinking, like he's staring straight through me, sizing me up, analyzing every breath.

He has a yellow legal pad in his lap, and when he sees me glancing at it, he bends it slightly upward so I can't make out what's on it. I have something in my lap too—a folder that holds a résumé, a community project idea, and a Bible study curriculum—things I brought to this meeting to show him who I am and what I can offer the church. But I never open it. For years, the crease of that folder will remain in the same position at the bottom of a tote in my closet. A relic of the moment my life fell apart.

I pour out my life to him. I share my hopes, my dreams, my struggles, my skills, my willingness to serve if only he will have me. He doesn't blink. Doesn't smile. Doesn't nod. He folds his hands over his notepad and says, "Let's pray."

My heart starts racing, my face is flushing—all the warning signs in my body screaming, "DANGER," because that didn't sound like a casual "Let's pray." It sounded more like, "Let's invite Jesus into this room, because something heavy is about to happen here." He prays, opens his eyes, purses his lips, and says, "I'd like to present you with some evidences I've collected over the past few months."

Evidences. Maybe I'm imagining his nostrils flaring and his lips snarling, but he delivers the word like he's been eagerly preparing to stab me with it. What evidences? I've only talked to this man once or twice and he has evidences? Of what? How long has he been watching me?

I hold my breath as he takes one in, and what flows out is what feels like a steady, unrelenting riptide of accusations. He doesn't stutter or emote; he simply lists the things I've done wrong and why I'm disqualified from ministry because of them. The words flow effortlessly, but they don't feel practiced. He speaks as if he has embodied this narrative, these *evidences*, and I'm not sure which is worse. I am caught in the undertow of his vitriol, every word another wave hitting me and taking me under, filling my lungs with water, drowning me in a fluorescent office.

I am breathless as he attacks me where I am most vulnerable: my motherhood. One of my children is unruly, he tells me. ("The other two are great!" he assures me.) He tells me that my basement is messy (but the rest of my house looks great!), and that's something he doesn't want leaking into the children's ministry. "If you don't teach your kids to clean up their playroom, they'll destroy the church too. He leans forward, saying, "I can't have someone serving in this church that can't control their children." He quotes Scripture about deacons being in control of their household and that my kids need to obey when my husband looks at them. That Zach shouldn't have to speak; they should "fall in line" to the sound of his voice. But my kids are too young to obey at a glance. I beg him to tell me what I'm supposed to do. I try to explain that the child he thinks is the problem is being tested for hearing loss and an auditory processing disorder. He shrugs. I ask him for advice, and he refuses. He just keeps repeating Scripture to prove I'm unqualified, but I'm confused because I'm not a deacon. It's stupid to ask the person holding your head underwater to throw you a life preserver, but I'm desperate. I want to scream, "Just tell me how to fix this!"

I'm out of breath, clawing for the surface. I'm disoriented, thrashing. This doesn't feel right, but he's so convincing. I must be wrong, because he has the Bible on his side. Our place in this church is hanging by a thread because I'm a bad mother. He didn't need to form the shape of the words with his mouth—I feel the threats in the stillness, the stare, the unspoken verdict hanging in the air. The implications are mine to understand and his to deny. I think I know what he's asking of me, but I need to hear him to say it.

I beg him, one last time, to help me. I believe him. I believe that I'm a bad mother and I *want* to be better. I want to stay. He sighs and says, "I'll tell you what I would do." Water fills my lungs for the last time.

He tells me to take a branch from a tree and make a switch. "It hurts enough to teach them a lesson but not enough to leave a mark." He tells me to switch my three-year-old. "Ten times a day, if need be."

I try to gasp, but there's no air for me to breathe anymore.

He narrows his eyes. "You have to break their spirits, Kristen."

He would know about that.

He has broken mine.

Breaking my children's spirits is the price of our ministry. It's the price to have a seat at this table. And it's not an option. I love their spirits. The last thing I would ever do is break them. I will not pay his price.

This final wave takes me under. I leave shaking, pale, barely able to put one foot in front of the other.

My husband greets me outside with a smile that quickly disappears. He reaches out to steady me. We drive home in silence. I know I'm going to have to tell Zach what just happened, but I can't yet. If I let the words rise to the surface, they'll start to breathe, and right now, I need them to drown with me.

One day I'll look back on this day with the righteous anger that comes with clarity, but right now, I just feel ashamed. This is my fault. I am bad. I am broken. I ruin everything. My poor husband and children. If only I was better. Why can't I be different?

Every building block I built my faith on has just crumbled beneath the weight of his evidences. In the aftershocks of this earthquake, my house of faith is turned into ruins. I can feel the ground shifting under my feet, threatening everything that used to feel unshakable. In this moment, I have no idea what this will mean for us. All I can think is that I've just ruined our lives.

The Meeting, as Zach and I have come to call it, was the catalyst for a lot of changes in my life, but it wasn't the first or last thing that happened. It was just the last straw. In the weeks that followed, we decided to leave. At that point, he exercised more and more control over our lives. We weren't to leave town on our days off without his permission. I was told to stay home with our children instead of attending events. At one point, he made Zach individually hand-wash every toy in the nursery at a specific temperature, in a specific way, because he'd heard that our son (who, by the way, was too old to be in the nursery) had thrown up—at home, a week earlier. The absurdity of it would be funny if it wasn't so calculated.

But his most invasive power play happened when he called Zach into his office and presented his tithing reports and demanded that we back-pay the one percent of our tithe that appeared to be missing. It didn't matter that we always gave above and beyond our tithe; we just didn't always label our envelopes. We had to pay up.

He'd call Zach into his office and ask if I'd been a part of certain conversations with other women. "Have you heard anything about *dissension*?" he'd ask.

He'd position his body in front of me when he saw me chatting with other people, abruptly stopping my conversations and staring at me silently until I walked away. High control. High stress. High fear. He had all the chips. We were just trying to survive.

In those chaotic and confusing weeks, I tried to make sense of what happened without the language to define it. One day a friend texted me a link to an article and said, "Read this. This sounds a lot like what just happened."

I read the article feverishly, as if it was going to save my life. It was my oxygen mask after the depressurization of my life. "One definition of spiritual abuse is: 'the mistreatment of a person who is in need of help and support or increased spiritual empowerment with the result of weakening, undermining or decreasing that spiritual empowerment.'"[1] It went on to list a few elements of spiritual abuse, and I mentally checked the boxes as I read:

- Pressure to conform . . . Check.
- Enforced accountability . . . Check.
- Censorship . . . Check.
- Manipulation . . . (How many checks are too many?) Check.
- Requirements for secrecy and silence . . . Check. Check.
- Misuse of sacred texts or spiritual teachings to control the person . . . Check.
- Requirement of obedience to the abuser . . . Check.

I excitedly sent the article to my husband. Not because I was thrilled about the reality we were living in, but because now we knew what this was. There's a very specific kind of relief in knowing that other people have been through what you've been through. There's ministry in bearing witness, and not only did that article bear witness to my pain, it also gave me words to talk about it.

The term *spiritual abuse* is fairly new, but the concept isn't.[2] The abuse of Scripture by people in positions of authority is as old as Scripture itself. However, it's only recently that researchers have started to study what it does to a person's body and mind, and the impact it has on communities. Not to state what's probably obvious, but . . . it's not great. Some studies have found that spiritual abuse can be more damaging to a person's mental health than *any* other type of abuse.[3]

We've only begun to scratch the surface of what religious abuse does to our minds and our nervous systems.[4] But here's what we know: When you're harmed in a spiritual environment, it rewires your entire operating system. This goes deeper than being frustrated with a system, a pastor, a person, or a theology. Spiritual abuse is systematic and targeted harm.

When your belief is bruised or, in some cases, *brutalized*, you may be unable to separate the people who hurt you from the framework of beliefs that weaponized their attack. You might come to false conclusions about the character of God. Why would you want to have anything to do with a God who would endorse the breaking of a child's spirit? Why would you seek a God who belittles your worth, fills you with shame, and condemns every step you take? You can only take so much before you get tired of trying to please a God who's never pleased.

After we left our church, I spiraled. It was so destabilizing to me that I was afraid to write about what was happening to my faith, even privately, in a journal. When something is just in your head, it's safe, in a way. You don't have to engage with it. You don't have to think about how it will affect your life. You can push it back, drown it out. It's only when you say the words or write them down or put them into the atmosphere in some way that they become real . . . and a problem.

The pieces of my faith that fell apart shattered my sense of belonging, but even more than that, they shattered my identity completely. Who was I, if not in ministry? Who was I, if not a sold-out, on-fire Jesus freak? Who was I, without Jesus? Would Zach want to leave me? Would my parents cut me off? Would my siblings still want me in their lives? If my beliefs went away, how much of my life would go with them?

It took me several years to come to terms with how my faith had changed. Every belief I'd felt certain of turned into sand and slipped through my fingers. I knew everything until I knew nothing. But even after all the sand had settled and I'd built a new house of faith, I still felt shackled by fear. I wasn't afraid that I was *wrong*; I was afraid of what changing my mind would cost me.

Nothing has been more disorienting than the loss of certainty in my faith.

I started my work with people who have been disillusioned or wounded by the church in 2019. At the time, *church hurt* was the most common term to use, but I quickly retired that from my vocabulary. I found it to be dismissive, often used with air quotes, as if it's some imaginary thing that holds no weight. "Church hurt" was treated as a "wittle church boo-boo," minimizing the injury and absolving the perpetrator from any and all wrongdoing.

But church hurt—or, more accurately, spiritual trauma—isn't a flesh wound; it's a systemic parasite that harms not just individuals but entire communities. It's an aggressive injury that requires acknowledgment, treatment, and accountability to heal.

The reason the wounds that happen in spiritual communities cut us in such deep ways is the same reason the loss of certainty in faith is so disorienting: When faith and community are intricately intertwined, the unraveling of one often means the unraveling of the other. Loss of community often leads to a loss of faith. And a loss of faith often leads to the loss of your community.

When you're a part of a faith community for any amount of time, you quickly learn which beliefs are acceptable and which are not. When you're "in," you know who's "out." And you also know what the in-group says and thinks about the out-group. That's all well and good when your beliefs fall within the threshold of tolerance for your community. But when you start to pull at the thread of a curiosity or a question, you know better than anyone else what's at stake.

Just as children learn social behavior by observing and imitating other people, we learn Christian social behavior by being in community and doing the same as those around us. We learn through systematic teaching, sure. But we learn even more by being with and engaging with other people.

We hear a conversation, we absorb it, we rationalize it, we process it, and we metabolize it into our spiritual nervous systems. We learn what words and behaviors keep us safe. We observe our community's response to someone who's in pain, someone who's questioning, someone who shares something vulnerable, and our brain subconsciously sets up defenses for us. If someone shares something vulnerable and is met with opposition or criticism, our brain tells us it isn't safe to be honest. We make subconscious notes to avoid experiencing humiliation and rejection.

I remember sitting in a women's ministry event about a year after we left. My friend leaned over and whispered, "Dude, are you okay?"

I said, "Yeah, I'm fine—what do you mean?"

She raised her eyebrows and pointed to my foot that was bouncing so hard I'm surprised I didn't take flight. My body was physically reacting to what my mind had perceived as a threat—something I couldn't really grasp or name at the time because I didn't know what spiritual trauma does to your brain. You aren't just experiencing hurt feelings, you're being completely rewired.

Here's what's happening in your brain:[5]

1. Pain centers are activated. Social rejection activates similar brain regions as physical pain.[6]
2. The amygdala, the part of the brain that's responsible for processing emotional stimuli, becomes more reactive to potential threats after experiencing rejection. This is what leads to hypervigilance and a tendency to interpret neutral situations as threatening.
3. The hippocampus, the part of the brain involved in memory formation, creates associations between vulnerability and the experienced negative outcomes. That influences how we engage relationally in the future.
4. Rejection triggers the release of stress hormones like cortisol, which can lead to heightened emotional responses and decreases our ability to change our mind or consider nuance.
5. Positive social interactions activate the brain's reward system, releasing oxytocin. This makes us want to repeat the behavior, hoping for the same results. However, when vulnerability is met with criticism, this reward response is depleted and has the opposite effect. Now we're not as willing to be open with people.

The evangelical church is not always a safe place for the wounded and the doubters. There might be a time limit. Sure, you can wrestle ("We all do!"), but eventually you need to arrive at some certainty. In unsafe communities, a lack of certainty signals two things: a lack of faith or an unwillingness to surrender some aspect of your life. "Just believe!" they tell you. "Just read your Bible!"

But faith doesn't work like that, does it? We can't muscle ourselves into belief. We can't will ourselves into a relationship with Christ. The church can coerce you into good behavior, but it can't pressure you into faith. Faith isn't something that can be bought, forced, or regulated. In many ways, faith is indefinable.

Go on a journey with me for a second. Let's say there's a small group, and one night an older gentleman—we'll call him Ben—feels safe enough to tell the group that he's struggling to believe in the, oh, I don't know, let's say the seven-day literal creation story. The room gets tense, because in this community, if you don't believe the world was created in seven days, you undermine the entire Bible, which undermines the entire story of God and his people. Without seven literal days, they believe you're without Christ.

Ben knows that, but he's turning to this group of people he loves and trusts to help him sort out his questions. He's searching for certainty and hoping that because they know him, they'll give him the benefit of the doubt. But instead of guidance, he receives a nervous deflection from the group leader.

"You know, Ben, having questions is totally normal, but we have to be careful not to let doubts lead us astray. Watch out for that slippery slope, buddy!"

The group giggles, and the discussion moves on.

But now Ben is embarrassed and a little scared. *Is it okay that I'm not sure about this?*

Ben continues on his journey of faith, and the more he studies and searches for answers, the more questions he has. Even though he knows he might get shot down, he keeps asking, because he can't keep it in. He wants to understand; he wants to know God; he wants his faith to strengthen and deepen.

But Ben's questions become a problem for the community. He gets tired of being humiliated by leaders who deflect his questions and minimize his doubts. He stops going to small group. He's less and less a part of the community until eventually he disappears from it.

"It's a shame about Ben," they say.

"Yeah, really is. He was such an overthinker. He just couldn't accept the truth."

"If only he'd stayed in our small group. We could have helped him!"

Ben was welcome to be a part of the community—until he wasn't. Once he stepped beyond what was tolerable for the community, he was passively pushed aside. We all have a Ben in our communities, or we've *been* the Ben. The harm is not only in what was done and said to Ben but also in the message being sent to the community at large. We see how the Bens are responded to—dismissed, vilified, bad-mouthed—and our brains internalize a protective message: *If you want to belong, don't tell the truth. Don't question. Don't push. Fall in line. Smile. Be nice. Don't be messy.* But how can we grow and mature if we aren't welcome in spaces where growth and maturity are fostered?

Fear of isolation bottlenecks the pursuit of truth. You feel the questions—they burn your throat—but you stuff them down, freeze them out, because if they dare to escape your lips, you'll lose belonging.

Faith that's been bruised is more than a personal struggle; it's a relational liability.

I've always struggled with knowing what's okay to say out loud and what's better left inside my head. I've been labeled rude, obnoxious, inappropriate. You know—all the ways women really love to be labeled. When talking about it with my therapist, he asked me if I thought this was because of my neurodivergence, and that could very well be the culprit, but I don't think it's only that. I think it's because I never genuinely consider that what I'm saying might be radical, awkward, or poorly timed. It just never occurs to me, *This might not be the place, Kristen.* Not until the words are already airborne and I'm mentally drafting my apology before anyone realizes what I just said.

I took a semester off college after my freshman year. I was really craving friendship, so I got involved in a young adults group at a church not far from where my parents lived. I was eighteen and very much in the differentiation stage of development. I have endless gratitude to Mark Zuckerberg for waiting until my prefrontal cortex fully formed before taking Facebook to the level it is today, because the world did not need eighteen-year-old Kristen on social media. The digital footprint would have been a monstrosity. As it were, I left my mark on this small group of kind, compassionate, introverted young people by being outspoken and obnoxious and maybe a tiny bit arrogant.

We read *Blue Like Jazz* together, and I was always the first one with thoughts to share. One night I said something particularly salacious, and everyone around the table went completely silent. The guy sitting next to me chuckled and said, "Well, we were all thinking it—she just *said* it." Everyone laughed and chimed in, and I felt proud of myself for saying the thing everyone wanted to say and making them feel safe to speak their minds.

I sort of adopted that characteristic and defined myself by it. I was a truth teller, and I came by it honestly. My dad is one too, to his own detriment at times. He's not the kind of pastor you think of when you think of pastors. He isn't particularly warm or gentle. He's a man of few words and always has been. When he preaches, you feel nostalgia for a time when church was a family affair that you dressed up for and stayed for hours afterward, gossiping with the church ladies at the potluck over what someone said during testimony time. And if you're looking for a pastor who will hug you and give you tissues while you cry into his chest, he's probably not your guy. But what you will get is the truth—about your situation, about what he thinks, about what the Bible says, about what he thinks that means. He won't lie, he won't sugarcoat, and he won't patronize. He doesn't even conceal the truth for his own benefit. I think that's really brave.

The biggest lies I've ever told, and the most harmful ones, have been about who I am and what I believe and think.

You don't realize how much you lie until you know someone who *never* lies. As much as I respect and look up to my dad's honesty, and as much as I emulate that myself to an uncomfortable degree, I don't tell the truth as much as he does. The biggest lies I've ever told, and the most harmful ones, have been about who I am and what I believe and think. My reputation for "saying it like it is" or "saying what everyone else is thinking but is afraid to say out loud" has provided me a measure of invisibility for the things I don't want to reveal about myself. If everyone thinks I always say what I'm thinking, if everyone thinks I publish every thought or struggle I've ever had, they're less likely to pry further.

This was especially true during the season of my life when my faith was falling apart. I knew what was at stake. I knew exactly which relationships would dissipate if these people knew what was going on inside me. I've never been good at hiding what I'm thinking. My face has subtitles, as they say. If I don't want people to see me or know me, I disappear, lest my face give me away.

When my faith was fracturing, I isolated myself. Every now and then, a crack would open in the curtain, giving people a glimpse at what was really happening, and my worst fears would be realized. Someone would leave, cringe, distance themselves from me, gossip during the potluck about me.

One of the best things about having community is that they're always there and in your business when you need them, but that's also the worst thing when your community isn't safe or is unwilling to accept you at a particular stage of faith. They'll be there, all right. But with panic and fear. "Ooh, that's a slippery slope." "You have to be careful. You sound bitter." There are rules, parameters, fears, warnings. The road is so littered with "DO NOT ENTER" signs that eventually all you can do is stand in place and scream.

I didn't need people yelling at me and warning me about the dangers of a wobbly faith. I already knew that. I needed a shepherd to lead me out. Their voices were telling me that my questions and my anger and my doubts were preventing me from "finding God," but that wasn't true. *They* were. When your compass is broken, you don't need a panicked passenger screaming warnings about everything that could happen to you. You need a calm guide. They were so afraid of what was happening inside of me, they couldn't see that the path I was taking would lead me to a faith that was beautiful, sincere, and deeply rooted. They kept me at arm's length, cautious of my questions and wary of the voices I was listening to. They threw up their hands and backed away slowly. *Whoa, whoa, whoa, buddy.* They opted out, and I was left to spiral on my own.

Fear. It all comes down to fear, doesn't it? I was afraid to voice my doubts because I was afraid of what it would mean for me spiritually and relationally. Many of the people around me were afraid that my questions would lead me to abandon my faith. I was desperately trying to hold *on* to it, and they were desperately trying to prevent me from losing it. Instead of pressing forward toward Jesus, I withdrew even more. I could feel myself fracturing from the inside out, and I thought it was my fault. I assumed it was my questions that were breaking me, my lack of faith, my lack of discipline. I never considered that this was a normal part of the journey of faith. I never considered that on the other side of this uncertainty, I would be okay.

Brian McLaren categorizes this into a four-stage model of faith development.[7]

STAGE ONE: SIMPLICITY

This stage is characterized by simple, clear-cut answers and a belief that everything is known or knowable. People in this stage tend to categorize things as right or wrong, good or bad.

STAGE TWO: COMPLEXITY

During this stage of faith, a person moves beyond dualistic thinking and is open to different perspectives. People in this stage allow for more nuance and recognize that there are other valid viewpoints, but they rely heavily on spiritual authority.

STAGE THREE: PERPLEXITY

This stage includes a lot of questioning and doubt. There is heavy skepticism, relativism, and a belief that nothing can be known. People in this stage are often angry and tend to be uncomfortably honest about their frustrations, doubts, and questions.

STAGE FOUR: HARMONY

The final stage of faith happens when a person reaches a place of peace with the known and the unknowable. People in this stage are marked by compassion, empathy, and love.

Philip Yancey talks about stages of faith as well, using developmental language. He categorizes the stages into three milestones: child (simplicity), adult (complexity), and parent (harmony).[8] To get a broad picture of the range of experiences in faith, I think both models are important. It's helpful to remember that we don't all fit into neat categories of faith, and we don't necessarily move through them in a linear way.

Learning about these stages helped me normalize what I was experiencing. It removed panic and allowed me to focus on growing and learning and maturing in my walk with Christ. Knowing that what I was going through was common enough for multiple people to name it and categorize it helped me feel less threatened by the process. It moved me out of the freeze state and into curiosity and the free pursuit of truth.

For way too long, I lived a life of broken and bruised faith because I valued preserving my social safety over having a sincere faith. I preferred to lie and deny my doubts than risk losing my belonging. I preferred the approval of my spiritual community over God's presence.

I know I'm not alone in this. How many of us are living fractured lives, hiding what we actually believe, afraid that honesty will cost us our friendships, families, and church communities? We smile, nod, and say the right things, but inside we're fractured. The risk of telling the truth feels too great.

It *is* a risk. And not a small one.

Some of us grew up in environments where asking questions equaled rebellion, doubting was spiritual failure, and stepping outside the norms of the community meant being expelled from it. When faith is built on certainty rather than, I don't know, *faith*, there's no space for wrestling, for mystery. There's only the weight of maintaining an image.

Some of us learned that God was only interested in our obedience. We learned that above anything else, he is a Judge ready to punish us for the slightest misstep. So we live fractured lives, never knowing what it means to have a faith that's been bruised and healed within a safe, loving, non-anxious spiritual community.

> A faith maintained through fear isn't faith at all—it's captivity. And Christ came to set us free from that kind of imprisonment.

Despite what you may have heard, God isn't standing behind a giant bench with a gavel, giddy to condemn you. That image, that perception of him, is a false one. God is more than Judge. In fact, it's not his goal for anybody to perish, but for *everyone* to be with him forever.[9] We're the ones who get so caught up on who's in and who's out.

God is kind, loving, patient, compassionate, caring, long-suffering, just, good, and 100 percent *for* you. Your doubts don't anger him. When Thomas, one of Jesus' disciples, didn't believe he'd actually risen from the dead, Jesus stretched out his hands and said, "See for yourself." Weird. He didn't even mention a slippery slope.

So maybe the question isn't "What happens to my relationships if I'm honest?" but "What will happen to me if I'm not?" A faith maintained through fear isn't faith at all—it's captivity. And Jesus didn't come to keep us chained up. He came to set us free.

I've come to believe that God doesn't demand my blind faith. He isn't the man sitting in his chair, towering over me and listing his evidences against me. He doesn't demand my certainty, and he doesn't weaponize my doubt. He walks straight into my questions, hands extended, and says, "See for yourself."

4

WWJD? He'd Like You

The Good News of Your Belovedness

GOLDEN GIRLS RETREAT, KANSAS CITY, MISSOURI, 2018

I'M SITTING AT A TABLE FULL OF WOMEN in a room full of women, feeling completely out of place. I don't belong here. I feel like an impostor. Everyone in this room is so cool, so beautiful. They are rich, stylish, mature, and out of my league. *God, what I wouldn't give to be one of them.*

I glance around and see a woman I recognize. Leslie. We only know each other from the internet and have had only a few brief interactions in comment threads and group messages. I give her a little smile and she waves. I return my focus to the women at my table, and out of the corner of my eye, I see Leslie crossing the room. A few people stop her and say hi, but she puts her finger up and smiles and points in my direction. She walks up to my table, and I expect her to introduce herself to everyone, but instead, she walks right over to me. She kneels on the ground next to my chair and tells me she's so excited to finally meet me. She asks me questions, she likes my outfit, how was my trip. We chat for a few minutes, then she stands up, gives a little wave to everyone else at the table, and walks back to her seat.

She crossed a room to talk to me.

Someone crossed a room . . . to talk . . . to me.

I don't know what her motivation was. I don't know what she's thinking, I just know that this is something that's never happened to me before. I am the invisible one, the shadow, the person wondering if anyone else in the room really wants them there. Being around smart, successful women and feeling out of place is familiar to me. Being someone who is cross-the-room-worthy is not. This brief interaction just wiped a little smudge off the mirror through which I see myself. The reflection looks different. Maybe I'm not who I thought I was.

I think every family has a funny-fodder kid, and that was me—unapologetically. I was hilarious. (Still am, by the way.) But as a kid, I didn't always mean to be. I suffered from a chronic lack of common sense. I was clumsy and forgetful, asked silly questions, and did things that made people wonder what planet I came from. My dad would call me a space cadet. My mom would quip that I should have been born blonde. (Those were the days of blonde jokes. I'm sorry. We've evolved.) Every time I saw my uncle, he would scratch my head and say, "Know what this is? It's a brain sucker and it's starving!"

Even as a kid, I understood that the jokes weren't mean-spirited.

My family enjoyed me and my high jinks. I knew that and I liked the attention. But even as I laughed along, there was a little thought in the back of my mind, the little seed of narrative that when fed, grows into a core belief: *This is all I'm good for—a laugh.*

The denomination I grew up in had a Wednesday-night program for girls called Missionettes and a boy counterpart called Royal Rangers. It was essentially Girl Scouts and Boy Scouts . . . but with Jesus. We had to complete projects to earn badges, there were award ceremonies—it was a whole thing. I became the first girl in my family to drop out. I never attended a single award ceremony.

But it wasn't *entirely* my fault.

When I was eight years old, my Missionettes teacher was a woman named Mrs. Sonya, and I was 100 percent sure she hated me. Looking back, I think she didn't actually hate *me*; she hated my dad. But she sure took it out on me. I have vivid memories of her giving snacks to every other kid in class and skipping me, rolling her eyes at me, ignoring my raised hand, and refusing to answer my questions, as if I was invisible. But one day she said something so cruel that even at the ripe old age of almost-forty, it still stings.

She needed someone to go to the office—where I'd literally been living until a few weeks before—to make copies. I raised my hand to volunteer, because who better than the person who had slept next to the copier every night for months, right? She rolled her eyes and waved me forward. I was so excited to be given this responsibility and to prove that I was capable and responsible. Maybe if I did a really good job, she would like me!

When I reached her desk, I put my hand out so she could hand me the papers. She looked me up and down and said, "Never mind. You're too stupid to do this. Sara, you do it." Those words *You're too stupid* carved themselves deeply into the way I saw myself. *I'm too stupid. I'm not good enough. I don't deserve anything good.* Moments like that shape us. They create narratives about who we are and what we're worth.

Dan Siegel, a neurobiologist and therapist, talks about how the stories we tell about our lives shape who we believe we are. These stories become the scaffolding of our identity.[1] If our stories are rooted in shame, they distort how we see the image of God in us. The past doesn't stay there—it influences our present and our future, and the voices that shape us don't disappear, they echo. They settle into us and quietly tell us who we are.

But there's good news too. Siegel's research shows that when we take time to look at our stories honestly—especially the painful parts—and weave them together with truth and compassion, something shifts. We begin to heal. We grow more resilient, more connected, and more whole.

This concept is displayed beautifully in the movie *Inside Out 2*. Yes, we're jumping from neuroscience to Pixar, because sometimes a good animated movie can explain something better than a decade of therapy. In the movie, the main character, Riley, is a young teen going through the brutal "system upgrade" of puberty. Throughout the movie, she experiences a few significant moments, like helping a friend out of an embarrassing moment. The memory forms into a glowing orb that drops into the Belief System, forming strands that become the foundation for the way she sees herself. As the strands stretch out, Riley's voice echoes her new core belief: *I'm a good person.* But there are sadder moments too. When Riley really wants to be accepted and perform well and she comes up short, a new core belief forms: *I'm not good enough.*[2]

Without contrasting voices, our negative core beliefs define the way we see ourselves. My self-hatred as a kid and teenager prevented me from being able to see anything redeemable about myself. My journals are filled with the words, "Why can't I get it together?" across every era of my life. Feeling broken as a child and believing that it was my fault made it impossible for me to see God clearly, because I could only see how much I'd failed. I tried to die to myself. I tried to be a better person, a more "together" person. Someone who could be respected—a leader, a world changer. Heck, I would've settled for "not totally terrible." Comments like Mrs. Sonya's planted seeds of shame that grew in my life, unchecked, for years.

I saw my first ghost* when I was eight years old. My brothers and I were playing hide-and-seek in the backyard of our home in New Jersey, and I was "it." It was a warm summer day, the year before our lives unhinged at the hands of my dad's church. It's one of my favorite childhood memories, ghost notwithstanding. I sat on our deck and faced the house while my brothers ran off behind me. With my hands over my eyes, I counted to thirty.

"Twenty-eight . . . twenty-nine . . . thirty! Ready or not, here I come!"

I whipped around fast and immediately locked eyes with a little boy who was hiding behind the only tree in our backyard. His eyes got wider, as if he was surprised I'd turned around so quickly. He smiled and ducked behind the tree. He was smaller than my

* Yes, there were more. Overactive imagination, indeed. (Or did I have a gift? Who's to say?)

brothers, with brown hair instead of their blond and red, and he wore overalls, not the worn-out "play clothes" our mom insisted we wear outside. I thought maybe he was a neighbor kid my brothers had invited to join us while I was counting. I called out, "Come out, come out, whoever you are! I see you!"

I ran over to the tree and jumped behind it with a "Boo!" to scare the hider and . . . nobody was there. I remember registering that as weird, but things like that were common for me. I didn't think anything about it.

After I found both my brothers, I asked them where the other kid went. They had no idea who I was talking about. Overall Boy was one of many "realities" I saw as a kid that I could never convince anyone else were real. I have vivid memories of trees falling through windows, car accidents, people who never existed, worlds I'd never been to, colors I couldn't explain, creatures that aren't real.

This little piece of lore in my life didn't really make sense until I was much older. If you have an understanding of how ADHD presents in little girls, you probably just read all that and clocked something that nobody would have registered in the '90s. The combination of "active imagination" and "lack of common sense" in little girls is essentially a pre-diagnosis for ADHD.[3] Creating elaborate stories, never being fully dialed in to what's happening, and having a blurry line between fiction and reality weren't the symptoms of a liar (or a sinner!) but the trademarks of a child with an overactive mind. I couldn't control my imagination. My mind couldn't stop working, so in its understimulated state, it would fill the silence with scenes of its own making—invented worlds, imaginary children, dramatic scenarios, and alternate realities. And yes, often without my awareness or involvement.

When I described these scenarios (and the maladaptive daydreaming that developed as a more prominent coping mechanism in adulthood) to my therapist years later, it triggered her to suggest that my type of ADHD would be categorized as "inattentive." Did you know there were types? I didn't. This is the part of the description that really got me: "Inattentive ADHD is too often dismissed as spacey, apathetic behavior in children, or misdiagnosed as a mood disorder or anxiety in adults." I didn't know that a single sentence could recontextualize my entire life, but there it was.

The moment I shook hands with the belief that it was ADHD that caused my least favorite behaviors, not my personal, sinful choices, I was never the same. Over the next several years, I went through a few different medical experiences, tests, and bloodwork that showed I have actual genetic markers that often lead to an ADHD diagnosis. This wasn't something I chose, something that was forced on me, a trauma response, or anything within the boundaries of my control. I was just . . . made like this. That doesn't mean that every part of my ADHD feels holy or helpful. There are aspects that frustrate me, complicate my relationships, and make my life harder. But even so, I believe I was made like this on purpose. Nothing about the makeup of my brain is a fluke. It's not some cosmic slip of the pen.

For most of my life, the labels given to me (spacey, scatterbrained) were given through the lens that something was missing in me. But the more I learn to see myself through the eyes of the one who made me, the more I'm learning to accept that I was made like this intentionally by the God who knows what he's doing. Even the parts of me I used to resent carry traces of his image.

As important as this moment was for me, it wasn't the only revelation that changed my life and transformed the way I saw myself. Just as crucial as discovering God's love was learning that his love didn't depend on me getting everything right. He doesn't need me to "get it together." That was another shock to my spiritual nervous system—but in a good, regulating way. Like taking a cold shower during a panic attack. So much of what I thought it looked like to get my act together required me to change things about myself that either didn't need to be changed or *couldn't* be changed. My overactive mind wasn't a character flaw. I had let other people define me and my character and my integrity for so long, but now it was time to let God rewrite the narrative.

Some expressions of evangelicalism (and I am making the distinction here that this is not Christianity itself) teach that our humanity—our quirks, our desires, even our joy—needs to be eradicated for the sake of holiness. Certain faith frameworks encourage so much denial of self—and even death of self—that our erasure is elevated over our refinement. This goes way beyond killing the "sin nature" and crosses over into doing away with anything about us that isn't "Christian." We're led to believe that the goal of faith is for us to disappear into some perfected version of ourselves that we'll never attain.

We may feel like we have to justify everything we want to do or be or give or go, so we baptize our choices in Christian purpose. What if we sometimes do things just because we want to? Not because God told us to or because it fulfills a purpose or calling? Not because it's evangelistic or explicitly Christian? We forget that we were created as humans. We are not divine, and we are not called to live on an elevated plane of reality. We are, at the same time, finite and infinite. And because of that, everything we do has Kingdom significance. We are eternal and we are the Kingdom.

What matters more is not the specifics of our life, but our character, our hearts and minds, how we live and move through life, how our character is aligned with Christ's. This can either set us free or stress us out, but every decision we make doesn't have to be the right one.

Shortly after I graduated from college, I was offered a job as a junior high youth pastor at a megachurch near Seattle, Washington. Zach and I were newly married, living in central New York at the time, and an offer like this wasn't something to sneeze at. A professor of mine had sent my name to the church, advocated for me, and pretty much secured the job for me before I even knew about it. The truth of it is, I didn't want the job because I was afraid to move away from my family. I wasn't ready. I overspiritualized it as much as a person could, but in the end, it was fear that drove my decision.

My professor called me one day and said, "Look. You can take this job that everyone in your graduating class would have *fought* for and God will be with you, or you can stay in New York with your parents and God will be with you too. His presence and approval aren't dependent on what you decide."

Looking back, I kind of regret not taking the job. It might have been really great or it might have been awful—I'll never know. But my professor was right. We won't derail our lives if we turn to the right instead of to the left. You can take the job or not take the job. You can pick the blue shirt instead of the red one.

I used to live my life frozen, waiting for God to confirm or deny every little movement. I wanted him to write it in the sky, to send someone to talk to me. I needed to be in the exact will of God, not the "permissive will."* I needed to feel something or hear something, so I lived mostly in indecision, afraid to do the wrong thing—which meant I did nothing. I still struggle with that.

But the "right" choice isn't always clear. God doesn't always give us a sign. But he has given us wisdom and discernment and instincts. When our life is rooted and sourced in him, every decision is made with him. When we live and move and have our being in him, our faith is integrated into our instincts. We move with him, wherever we go. We don't need to move only in Christian spaces or for hyperspiritual reasons. When our faith is embodied, we don't need a formula or a checklist.

When our faith is embodied, we don't need a formula or a checklist.

When we know who we are in Christ, we understand that we are loved and *liked* by the one who made us on purpose. A Christianity that makes us feel guilty for existing or like we need to hide the things that make us *us* is rooted in fear, not the love of God. It seeks to control our identity, not help us see the reflection of God in it. It demands that we align with certain parameters for who we're allowed to be rather than allowing us to shine the light on who God has made us to be.

I had to break up with Christian culture to fall in love with Jesus again. The culture I was in was suffocating me. I couldn't move without criticism. I couldn't keep track of all the things I

* The "permissible will of God" is the idea that God has a perfect will for each of our lives, but we don't always make the decisions we need to make to achieve that perfect will. In this case, there is his *permissible* will, which is not his ideal for us but a diversion he allows in his grace. Because nothing says *unconditional love* like divine disappointment.

was supposed to do and be and like and talk about. I couldn't separate what was my "sin nature" from what was hardwired in me, and I got tired of trying to figure out how to win the affection and attention of my heavenly Father. I didn't need to. I never did. But I felt so much pressure from the communities I was in to present my "best self" to the King. I wasn't sure what that best self even was, so I overanalyzed everything I did. I didn't know who I was because I didn't understand who God wanted me to be. I was so lost.

I had to break up with Christian culture to fall in love with Jesus again.

When we talk about identity, it's important to recognize that we don't become who we are in a vacuum. We don't wake up one day with everything we'll ever be neatly wired into our personality. We are born, but we also become. We are products of the voices in our lives, the environments we spend time in, and the people we're surrounded by. We aren't static creatures. We change, we grow, we adapt, we become.

We were created to live in community with other people, and we need other people to help shape our healthy development. Children need adults who love them, nurture them, and call out their goodness. When a child's first identifiers are *bad*, *sinner*, and *wicked*, that may become the only way they see themselves as adults—and, consequently, the way they see other people. Children inherently believe anything the adults in their lives tell them. If you tell a kid they're bad, they'll believe they're bad. The harm this causes is undeniable and has lasting implications. As beings who were created for community, we have a fundamental need for relationships. When those relationships harm our identity, it changes the way we function in the world.

Zach and I recently put our kids in public school for the first time, after homeschooling them their entire lives. It probably goes without saying, but it's been . . . an adjustment. Our middle schoolers come home from school and sometimes act like Zach and I are enemy operatives and they've been briefed to act like jerks at any cost to make us crack. We look at each other with our eyes wide and coregulate like our lives depend on it (and they probably do). Instead of yelling at the kids, we silently agree that what's happening here is a case of body snatchers. These aren't our kids rolling their eyes and snapping at us—it must be somebody else. So we say something like, "Hey, you're not acting like yourself right now. What's going on?" If the body-snatcher behavior persists, we tell them to take a break in their room until they can figure out how to evict whatever alien entity took over their body and get it back. It works about 47 percent of the time.

I've shared some of these stories with a friend who grew up in an abusive, hyperconservative Christian home. He's grown up and found a way to heal in spite of all the ways he was mistreated. He's stronger and braver than he'll probably ever acknowledge, but he's told me that seeing the way we parent our kids with empathy and patience helps him to heal the parts of himself that never experienced that kind of emotional safety.

Positive messaging toward children is crucial for healthy emotional development and attachment. It shapes the way they see themselves and the world around them. When children don't experience comfort, connection, or a sense of safety, it changes the way they grow. They learn to adapt, but not always in healthy ways. Some become hyperaware of other people's moods, always evaluating the temperature of the room to see if they're safe. Others might shut down their feelings completely, convinced that their emotions aren't welcome or safe to be expressed. As they grow, they might struggle to form close attachments with others, they might be more vulnerable to stress, and they might often react inappropriately to situations. School can be a struggle. So can jobs, friendships, and health—anything that requires trust, connection, and steadiness.[4]

The way children are cared for sets the course for their entire lives. When they are burdened with unreasonable moral and spiritual expectations before their brains are developed enough to comprehend them, it negatively impacts their sense of who they are and who God is to them. The messages they receive do lasting damage: *I'm bad. God is mad at me. I deserve to be punished.*

Some Christian communities have taken messages from Scripture like "Die to self" and overblown them until they become "Hate thyself." Anything that makes us human is seen as a weakness we're meant to kill. Developmentally appropriate behavior in children is viewed as proof of original sin. Our human existence is viewed with suspicion, zooming in on our flaws and imperfections and hyperfocusing on the parts of ourselves that need to be destroyed so we can be the version of ourselves we're "supposed" to be. But every time someone puts a crack in the foundation of our humanity, it fractures the image of God reflected in us.

We think that the more we cut away at ourselves, the more clearly we'll see God and the better he'll be reflected. But that isn't what happens. Instead, we become hypercritical of ourselves, and that critical spirit goes outward from there. We're judgmental of others because we're judgmental of ourselves. We hold others to high standards we can't meet ourselves. We secretly enjoy watching other people fail because it makes us feel better about our standing with God. At least we're not like that guy, right? We forget that God cast his image onto us when he created us, and he doesn't remove his likeness in us, no matter what we do.

We're intrinsically and unchangeably the reflection of the image of God. We all bear his image in our bodies, on our faces, in our genetic makeup. We're his by both spiritual birth and physical creation. This truth is a beautiful and sobering reality of our equity before the throne of God. The best and the worst of humanity are united in the reflection pool of God's glory.

When that image is fractured, whether by our own self-criticism or from the abuse of others, shame fills the cracks in our souls. Shame causes us to live in fear. And fear destroys our lives and our relationships. In *The Soul of Shame*, Curt Thompson describes shame as an emotional weapon that evil uses to destroy love and relationships. He says that when we allow shame to go unchecked in our lives, it doesn't just affect us individually. It spreads like a contagion through our relationships and communities.[5] Shame is a direct path to destruction. There are no exceptions.

Identifying the areas where we're viewing ourselves through the lens of shame is crucial to ending its reign in our lives. We have to learn how to actively notice it, acknowledge it, and take a sip of the antidote so shame stops bringing harm into our lives. The antidote to living in shame is to metabolize into our nervous systems how deeply we are loved by God.

When children grow up in homes where they know they're safe and loved, they're much more likely to grow into well-adjusted, mentally healthy, emotionally strong adults. The same is true when it comes to faith. If we think God is holding a hammer over our heads, waiting to punish us when we mess up, we'll live in fear.

Fear leaves no room for joy and peace. But when we believe that God loves us, *likes* us, and wants to be with us, we'll live into his promises to us: joy, peace, and abundance.

There's a powerful passage in Ephesians that I've been hooked on for years now. Paul is describing how powerful the love of God is:

> I pray that he may grant you, according to the riches of his glory, to be strengthened with power in your inner being through his Spirit, and that Christ may dwell in your hearts through faith. I pray that you, being rooted and firmly established in love, may be able to comprehend with all the saints what is the length and width, height and depth of God's love, and to know Christ's love that surpasses knowledge, so that you may be filled with all the fullness of God.
>
> **EPHESIANS 3:16-19**

In the entirety of Scripture, you won't find a single passage that describes God's wrath and judgment this way—as needing the strength of Christ and all the saints to even begin to kind of understand. His wrath isn't unknowable. His judgment isn't undefinable. But his love? Now that you'll need to sit down for.

Why do you think God's love is the thing we can't wrap our minds around? Why did Paul think this truth was so crucial for people to understand? Why did the churches pass down this letter until it was universally accepted as part of the story of God and his people? If the earliest fathers and mothers of the church thought that emphasizing the love of God was a threat to our holiness, the inclusion of this passage in the canon of Scripture is evidence to the contrary.

I think these words are some of the most important in Scripture because it isn't hard to believe we're worthy of punishment. It is, however, a challenge to believe that we're worthy of being loved. So much so that Paul says we need supernatural strength in our being, combined with the comprehension of all the saints, before us and around us, to even begin to know how deeply, truly, and securely God loves us.

God wants us to be "rooted and firmly established in love," not loosely aware of it. His love is not secondary to his wrath. It isn't a footnote in our lives. It isn't something we need to analyze, explain, define, or understand; it's just something that is ours. We don't need to get our act together to access that love. We don't need to fix ourselves up. We don't need to have a "better" brain. We don't need to do anything or be anyone other than who we are right now, in this moment. We are accepted, loved, and *cherished.* There are no exceptions to the love of God. There are no requirements. God loves you, likes you, and wants to be with you. Sometimes we forget this, and we make choices like scared children, afraid we'll get spanked if we choose the wrong thing. We detach from God's love and live from fear.

There are no caveats to the love of God. God loves you, likes you, and wants to be with you.

When I forget God's love for me, I start trying to prove my worth to other people. I become critical of other people's choices and behavior. I focus on everything that's going wrong. I believe that I'm alone and abandoned and that everyone, even God, is against me. I feel shame about everything, even things I have no reason to feel ashamed about. I hide and distance myself from other people. I project my feelings and my frustration onto others. I stop noticing the presence of God in my life because I'm afraid of what his presence will bring. Judgment? Rebuke? Shame? The risk is too high, so I hide.

But when I remember how deeply I'm loved, I'm more relaxed, more joyful, and more hopeful—even when hard things are happening. I don't feel personally attacked or easily offended in my interactions. I'm friendlier and more hospitable. I seek connection instead of avoiding it. I can handle hardships without complete devastation.

Moving through life "rooted and firmly established in love" means living from a place of trust, contentment, and hope. When we know that we're loved and that we're safe in that love, we don't worry that it will be taken from us. We don't have to overperform to be worthy. We don't try to convince everyone that we're good, the best, the holiest, because we know we don't have to be. We don't make decisions out of fear. We have more margin for wisdom and critical thinking. We're more creative, adventurous, and joyful—in a word, free.

When I look back at little me, I don't feel ashamed anymore. I used to reflect on my childhood and say things like, "My parents should have spanked me more," or "Man, God had so much grace on me because I was so *bad*." Knowing that God loves me and likes me allows me to view little Kristen with joy. She didn't need more discipline; she needed to believe that she was made in God's image and that God loved her. She didn't need a different mind or a different attitude; she needed to grow and mature and see herself through the eyes of God. I wasn't broken or bad. I was just little.

Sometimes I still want to say that. "I'm just *little*—don't be mad at me!" But maturing in Christ and relaxing into his love for me has also changed the way I respond to my mistakes. Without shame, I don't need to hide when I mess up. I can confess it, address it, acknowledge it, and apologize for it—not because I'm afraid, but because the love of God changes the way I respond to everything, including my mistakes. Shame hides wrongs; love corrects them. Shame views the wrongs of others with contempt; love forgives them. Shame imprisons our minds and our bodies; love sets us free.

Why is it, then, that in some Christian traditions, when a person decides to follow Jesus, their primary identifier becomes "sinner"? Not "new creation." Not "the righteousness of God in Christ Jesus." Not "anointed," "set apart," "holy," or "chosen."[6] But . . . sinner. Why should we center our identity on what Christ already redeemed? Of course, it's important to recognize our flaws and weaknesses, but our primary identity in Christ is not *sinner*; it's *beloved*, *chosen*, and *transformed*.

If we identify as a sinner without also claiming our identity as God's righteousness, we're choosing to wear only the weight of condemnation. But it isn't Christ who condemns. In fact, the Bible says that there is *no condemnation* for those who are in Jesus. The moment we come to Christ shouldn't be the moment we become acutely aware and ashamed of our filth; it's the moment we become acutely aware of how loved we really are. This is the message and hope of the cross: that Christ has transformed us. He defeated death, sin, and shame. Why do we insist on identifying ourselves by the things he destroyed for us?

Since the very first humans curled their toes into the dirt of the earth, the enemy has been chipping away at our identity. The enemy's story is filled with lies and manipulation. He's bent on getting us to believe that we're something we're not and that our Creator isn't who he says he is. God is not the accuser. In fact, in the courtroom metaphor, Jesus is our attorney, advocating for our goodness. He calls us his children, his beloved, his righteousness.[7]

What we believe about our identity matters because it changes the way we live and move in the world. If we believe we're dirty, rotten sinners, we'll live that way. If we believe we're beloved and chosen by a God who not only loves us but *likes* us, we'll live from love, not fear.

Identity guides our actions, responses, relationships, and emotions. Who we are is how we see ourselves; it's what we're passionate about, what brings us joy, what makes us laugh, how we process information, how we communicate, what movies we like, what books we read.

If the goal in Christ is transformation, then we must, to some degree, be aware of ourselves.[8] Without an understanding of our identity, we adopt the identity of our community, leaders, and the people we look up to. When those people fail, or when we leave our communities, our identity suffers. When our identity is fractured, we can no longer see God clearly. We can't reflect an image we can't see. When we have an identity that is formed by community but not staked in it, we won't be altered or bruised as deeply when the circumstances around us change.

I was shocked that a woman I respected crossed a room to talk to me, so imagine the shock of finally understanding that God has been crossing rooms to be with me since he breathed life into my lungs. Locking my spiritual eyes with the heart of God and seeing joy, acceptance, and pride helped me relax into my belovedness and open my heart to receive his love.

Life in Christ is full of *so much* good news. It's good news that shame doesn't have a rightful place in our lives, no matter what we've done. It's good news that what happened to us in the past doesn't have to define every moment of our future. It's good news that when we were created, God called us *good*. It's good news that his love is unfathomable and we will never get to the bottom of it.

You are a reflection of the glory of God, and that reflection is beautiful, good, worthy, and radiant. You can relax into the love of God and trust that you're safe.

5

Acquire the Fire, Survive the Burn

Metabolizing Spiritual Pain

COLD STONE CREAMERY, SPRINGFIELD, MASSACHUSETTS, 2019

MY DAUGHTER'S VOICE ECHOES in the bathroom of the ice cream shop while we wash our hands. As I adjust my clothes, she catches a glimpse of my shirt riding up over my stomach.

"Mom, is there a baby in your belly?"

"No, there's no baby in there anymore." I swallow the emotion her words have drawn to the surface. I scrub my hands vigorously under the rushing water, grateful to have something to focus on other than the grief her question just cracked open.

Her eyes stay locked on me, and she asks, "'Cause the baby died?"

There it is. I knew it was coming, but my chest tightens anyway and my eyes well up with tears. I stop the pain from stretching across my face. It isn't her fault. I don't want her to feel this too.

I force my lips into a smile. "Yeah, because the baby died."

She quickly responds, "So now you just have the belly and not the baby." She says it cheerfully, like she just said the right answer to "What's two plus two?"

I help her dry her hands, and she opens the bathroom door, skipping to her dad, leaving me to try to pull myself together at the sink. Her words were only innocent statements of the observable truth, but I'm pulling at my shirt as if it will tether me back to the ground that existed before our loss. I feel exposed, embarrassed by the body that couldn't sustain our baby's life, betrayed by the hormones and swelling that won't let go. I adjust my clothes around a belly that has no reason to be as big as it is—the baby was never big enough to need that much room anyway.

I find my family and sit down, stirring my ice cream around in the bowl until it melts.

Grief feels much like choking. One moment you're fine, ordering ice cream and wiping sticky hands, and the next you're frozen, your body remembering a grief you'd like to forget, your mind undoing everything you thought you'd already processed. Pain grows like vines over everything. Even the good things. It grabs and consumes everything it can until you can't remember how anything looked before sadness covered everything. When you look at a photo of someone you love who is gone, you can never look at the photo the same way again. You'll never only feel one thing. Every memory captured is also a reminder that they aren't here anymore. Every smile has a shadow of sadness behind it.

The vines grow out of control for a while, and you let them.

They may get closer and closer to your throat, but at least they're hiding you. At least it's dark here and you don't have to see the rest of the world seemingly living without vines. For a time, you stretch your arms wide and let them grow up around you, wrapping themselves around your pain until it feels less like a threat and more like a hug. You learn to live with the memories, the pain, the gut punches. You get used to feeling out of breath. Until one day, you don't feel the vines anymore.

The tendrils that used to choke you grow over your pain, covering you with the kind of life that grows when you don't cut it back. Over time, the vines turn something hidden into something flourishing. People stop and say, "Wow, look how beautiful." Like a weathered old building whose brick peeks out through the green. You become something different, something beautiful, because of something that grew where it wasn't supposed to grow. The vines are the scars of our pain, marking the places our lives have been touched by the unthinkable, proof that we survived.

It's a strange experience to carry your loss in your body. To wear it in your skin, stretched over an empty stomach that hasn't got the memo it's empty yet. No one can see the scars of a loss like that. But they're there regardless.

My body is covered in all kinds of scars. Most of the ones you can see are from stupid things. I have one on my right wrist from the time I was spinning in my friend's living room with my arms outstretched until my hand caught the edge of her metal stair railing. I have a matching pair on my knees, from two different occasions of falling on hot asphalt. I have one on my ankle from being pushed off a diving board I was taking too long to jump from. I have one on my left thumb from trying to put a hole in my belt with a knife . . . while *wearing* the belt. I have one between my knuckles on the same hand from the same thing, because sometimes scars are teachers but the mind doesn't always keep the score as well as the body. I have one on my chin from trying to steady my brother's BB gun to set the trigger. It didn't catch all the way, and my chin caught the snap back.

Not all scars are unwanted, though. Some we get to choose. My C-section scar is one of those. It stretches across my belly, and although it took me over a year to look at it, touch it, or even think about it, I no longer resist what it asks me to remember. It stores trauma I wasn't ready to face at first, but now I see it as the mark of what love and sacrifice can cost.

The procedure was an emergency, but I'd made my decision weeks earlier. Because of some complications with their shared placenta, my doctors told me that my twins had to be born, at the very latest, at thirty-two weeks. After weeks of anxious research and conversations with the many doctors assigned to our case, I was confident that a C-section was the safest, lowest-risk way to get our daughters here safely. When my doctor asked me what I wanted to do, I said, "I want you to open me up and scoop my babies out as carefully as you can." When my body developed preeclampsia and went into labor at twenty-nine weeks, she asked me one last time, "Do you want to consider vaginal delivery? I've done it this early before."

"Absolutely not," I said. "Scoop them out as carefully as you can."

My daughters lived and grew and healed in the NICU for a couple of months. We were so fortunate to bring them both home, and now the scar tells the story—of my decision, of our survival—and it serves as proof that I can heal from both physical and emotional trauma, because, Lord, did that story hold a lot of both.

Scars are proof that we healed, and they're reminders that we're capable of healing again. If it can scar over once, it can scar over twice. There is unbearable pain in knowing that as truth. Because for better or worse, pain transforms us.

Like a toddler who learns not to touch a stove after getting burned, pain teaches us. It matures us, forces us to take roads that lead us away from who we thought we were and who we'd always be. Pain is a guide, a teacher, a catalyst. And although we would never choose it, it shapes who we are. The scars that are visible are a little easier to address. It's the ones that sit beneath the surface, slowly and indefinitely shaping the way we move through the world, that are harder to integrate into a healthy, well-formed life.

Before I understood the way trauma changes us and shapes us, I just thought I was a difficult person. I thought my trauma responses were character flaws, signs of weakness, or evidence of a lack of spiritual depth. I thought if I spent more time in prayer, if I sacrificed more, if I dug into the corners of my heart to confess all my secret sin, I'd suddenly be transformed into a person who could handle her life. But pain isn't something we can bootstrap our way out of. And it's not passive—it carves a path inside us. We can follow the breadcrumbs and find the moments that shaped something in us.

If you're a people pleaser (meaning you have a pattern of setting aside your personal needs and wants to make other people happy, regardless of how it affects you), you weren't born that way. You developed this trait somewhere along the way because rejection left a mark on you. Maybe you were picked on for the music you liked or the clothes you wore, or maybe when you walked into a room, someone sighed like they didn't want you there. This could have been a pattern in your childhood, teaching you that approval has to be earned, that love is conditional, that belonging can be taken away. So now you want to keep people happy all the time, even if it's detrimental to your well-being.[1]

If you're anxious in your relationships, never knowing where you stand with another person and bracing yourself for rejection even when there's no sign of it, that's not because of your personality type or your astrological sign or your Enneagram number. It's likely because you have a scar called *abandonment*. Somewhere in your story, you were left alone, and this taught you to stay on high alert. Maybe someone you trusted left—physically, emotionally, or both. Maybe love always felt unpredictable, and now your heart doesn't just hope for security, it clings to it with a death grip, because losing it feels scary and unbearable.[2]

If you're emotionally reserved and controlled, you probably have a scar shaped like the person who made you believe that emotions aren't safe. Maybe you grew up in a home with a parent who was emotionally manipulative or explosive, and you learned that the only safe emotions were the ones that couldn't be seen or heard.[3] And now, as an adult, you might be the one who always seems calm and unbothered, but under it all is a heart that was never allowed to break without consequences. You don't open up easily, not because you don't feel deeply, but because it's never felt safe to do so.

These aren't quirks or habits; they're imprints of the wounds we carry.

The same pain that shapes our identity shapes the way we view ourselves. We create narratives about ourselves as a result of things that have harmed us. *She doesn't want to be friends with me because I'm annoying. He hit me because I keep nagging him. He doesn't love me because I'm ugly.* We form core beliefs around our wounds.

What happens when a wound heals improperly? Ask my crooked thumb.

Turns out, breaking your thumb and then saying, "Meh, they're not gonna do anything with it anyway," isn't exactly the best way to go about handling an injury. Not only do I have a thumb that is hilariously crooked, I also have pretty chronic thumb pain on my dominant hand, which is truly the worst kind of injury for a writer. Maybe if I'd seen a doctor, gotten a brace, let them set it and put some screws in it, I'd be all right. Or a little less crooked, at least.

Besides my thumb, I also live with chronic back pain—something I've dealt with since I was a teenager. There were a few injuries: a car accident, a truly unhinged child I was babysitting who kicked my spine in a fit of anger. That pain was tolerable until my C-section. Since then, my back pain has become something I have to deal with every morning. I wake up, I stretch, I roll my back out, I take medicine. It hasn't stopped me from living my life, but my fear is that one day it'll be too much, and I'll have to have surgery. I don't know what it's like to wake up without pain anymore. I can't remember the last time my body felt good, head to toe.

Humans are kind of amazing in that way. We adapt to pain and learn to live with it. When our pain heals over into scars, we learn to navigate life with them and we adjust to the way our pain and our scars have changed us.

Just like a broken thumb that doesn't get the right treatment to heal properly, spiritual malformation happens when something in our souls heals the wrong way. When a wound, whether physical or spiritual, doesn't get the right care, it doesn't just go away (outside of a miracle, of course). It causes us to adapt. It reshapes us. And it often leaves us with chronic spiritual pain we don't recognize as out of the norm anymore.

In our search to find meaning in our pain, we often force our experience to shake hands with a belief that *seems* to make sense. Like if a pastor tells us, "The reason this happened is because you lack faith, and here's a Scripture to back that up," we might metabolize what the pastor said without doing our own research or study or critical thinking on the matter. And we might allow his interpretation of a Scripture or event to become an absolute truth in our spiritual nervous system.

Our scars become liabilities when they heal over harmful beliefs, shaping not just how we see ourselves but how we think healing should happen. Which is especially problematic when these beliefs involve blaming the person who's hurting or attributing something nefarious to God's character. These false ideas perpetuate malformation and interfere with a person's healing. It's like giving someone an aspirin when they need surgery. It might take the edge off, but it doesn't heal the problem . . . and it might actually kill them. Part of transforming our pain and trauma into scars involves allowing ourselves to be marked and changed by the pain but not defined by it. Pain changes the way we navigate and engage with certain places, people, and aspects of our lives. Sometimes our experiences prompt behaviors that are reactive and protective, which may be necessary in the moment but harmful in the long term. If we continue to engage in behavior that is harmful for us or other people, our trauma is the *reason* for the behavior, but it isn't a justification for it. It's our unfair responsibility to repair damage we didn't cause so we don't perpetuate further harm. To repair, we have to take responsibility for our actions and behavior, *even if it's not our fault that we're this way*.

Our pain can be a weapon, or it can be a balm.

It isn't fair. It isn't right. But no one is responsible for our pain or our triggers except us. The world won't always accommodate us the way we need it to. And so, for our scars to remain scars and not become weapons in someone else's story or prisons that enslave us in the aftermath of pain, we need to learn to move through the world with pain as a passenger, not a driver. There comes a point in our healing journey when it becomes our responsibility to not make our pain the source of someone else's.

This is a tricky process to navigate. Healing has no timeline. When do we cross the threshold into responsibility? What's the "age of accountability" for our trauma responses? These are questions with no clear answers. Some days we're wounded, bleeding out, unable to control the bleeding. Other days we're on the defensive, and we become the ones who wound. The line between the two is thinner than we'd like to admit. We have to hold the tension between "I am the way I am because of my pain" and "My pain has caused me to react and respond in ways that aren't always healthy, and I'm actively taking steps to heal these wounds so I don't continue to cause hurt—to myself or others." When we find the strength to own the things that have happened to us, they stop being liabilities to our lives.

I'm raising two children who have nervous system regulation challenges, processing disorders, and developmental delays related to their prematurity. They're only four years old, but we have already been faced with the harsh reality of how unaccommodating the world is for them. Checking out at the grocery store is a terrifying experience for them. It always ends in them crying, screaming, and trying to throw themselves out of the cart. Church is so overstimulating that their nervous systems are completely fried within the first ten minutes. Going to large gatherings outside our home ends in us leaving early with two screaming toddlers and three disappointed older kids.

The world isn't made to match their needs, and you might be surprised at how many people are simply *unwilling* to accommodate. It's frustrating and it's hurtful. I have stomped my feet and cried and, at times, begged people to be understanding, to flex, to meet us where we are instead of requiring that we put our daughters in situations that are harmful for them.

Since the world will often refuse to make room for them, the best thing I can do for my daughters is to teach them how to navigate that world. I can teach them that they deserve compassion and kindness, but that they aren't guaranteed it. I can teach them how to advocate for themselves and encourage them to never doubt their worth. I can teach them how to weigh the risk when something will take a toll on their nervous systems and how to not feel broken or less-than when they don't have the same capacity as their friends. I can teach them that they are fearfully and wonderfully made and that nothing is wrong with them, while also acknowledging that the world may be easier for other people. They'll have to process their hurt, resentment, and anger—maybe for the rest of their lives. My job as their parent is to give them the tools to process in a way that's healthy, not destructive. They'll need to learn how to self-regulate, how to say no, how to educate other people about their needs, and how to ask for what they need.

I can't promise a world that will care for them. But I can teach them to care for themselves and each other, and how to find people who are safe, loving, and kind. They came into this world with trauma, and although our culture has taken huge strides in becoming more compassionate, the reality is that most of the world won't care about their struggles. They'll be expected to find their place, just like the rest of us, regardless of what they've been through. Is it fair? No, of course not. But it just . . . is. I can't help my daughters by promising them that the world will be different or by making them feel angry when it isn't different. I can only help them learn how to live in it.

We all have to learn to live with our scars and find the strength in them.

When I first started writing books, a lot of people assumed my first book would be about church hurt and spiritual abuse. That made sense. It's what I wrote about online, and my in-person ministry was with people who had been hurt by or disillusioned with the church. When the book I pitched to publishers was about trauma and suffering and the shared human experience of that, the response I received was sort of a collective . . . *Huh?*

I actually *did* write an entire book about church hurt. It's called *The Church Hurt You + I'm Sorry*, and it's in a document on my computer. It's a fully written manuscript that will likely never see the light of day—not in its entirety, anyway—because when I wrote it, I was writing myself out of the pit I'd been thrown into. By the time I was ready to publish a book, I didn't want to talk about the pain anymore; I wanted to talk about how I healed. Talking about your trauma brings you back into it, and I didn't want to stay in that pain anymore. I didn't want to become "the church-hurt girl." I didn't want to be identified by the things that broke my heart, derailed my life, and caused me the most pain. The trauma I experienced inside the walls of the church changed me indefinitely and dramatically. I am unrecognizable to the person I once was, but I don't want to be defined by that pain.

Because of the nature and content of my writing, much of my ministry involves sitting with people who have experienced unthinkable wounds in spiritual contexts and helping them process that pain. Sharing my story publicly in books, blog posts, Instagram stories, and podcasts has carved out a community of people who are hurting and want someone to listen to them without correcting them or spiritually bypassing their trauma.

Most of my days are spent listening. Sometimes it's over coffee. Sometimes it's through DMs, Zoom calls, retreats, writing courses, or workshops. Wherever it is, the stories find me. Stories of abuse—spiritual, sexual, marital, verbal, physical. Families who abandon children who have deconstructed their faith. Parents who block their child's phone number because they're gay. Children who cut off their parents. Pastors who cheat on their wives and are welcomed back into spiritual authority while their affair partners must leave and hide. Boards that conspire behind a pastor's back to fire him and force him out of his house, offering no severance and leaving him with no employment or home. These aren't outliers; these are stories I hear *every day*.

I don't think people tell me these things because I'm the world's best listener or because I dispense the sagest advice. I think it's because we run to people with matching scars. We know that they get it. They can hold space, offer compassion, listen, validate our pain, and honor our experiences without rushing us to get better. And that is a beautiful, sacred thing. When we share our story and how it has affected our life and someone says, "Same," our shoulders relax. We exhale and we realize we're safe.

Same is a love note. *Same* is a deep breath.

We flock to people who make it easier to navigate life with scars. For our own health and the health of our community, we need to become active participants in healing one another's pain. Healing often comes in the form of casseroles, "thinking about you" texts, and honoring another person's pain without commentary.

Community is an essential part of healing. It validates our pain to hear that other people have experienced the same things we have. When we see others who have walked ahead of us and shown us the way, it gives us hope that it's possible to reach the other side of pain. Of course, there's also a potential danger in making pain our primary identifier. It can radicalize us to the degree that it harms us and the people around us, until we find ourselves anticipating a monster in every pew. If we don't steward our pain well, the thing that unites us can become the thing that undoes us.

But it doesn't have to. When we steward our pain well, it can be the thing that binds us together in meaningful, life-giving ways. The difference is in the way we hold the pain. When we deal with our wounds with honesty and hope instead of anger and suspicion, pain becomes fertile ground for compassion, connection, and resilience.

There's a holy city in India called Vrindavan that has become a place of refuge for widows. In many regions of India, women aren't treated with fairness and dignity, and the loss of a husband means the loss of economic security and social stability. In some Hindu traditions, widows are not allowed to remarry, so their usefulness to society is essentially *nothing*. They're abandoned by their families and given over to a life of poverty, rejected by society and left to go through the rest of their lives in hardship. Every year, thousands of widows, with no other options, make their way to Vrindavan, where communities of widows are established and thriving.

Shunned and stripped of social and economic support, these women have built communities together. They share what they have with each other and assert their dignity, despite the way they've been viewed and treated by their society. Their lives have been deeply marked by pain and loneliness, but they've found a way to navigate a culture stacked against them. Inside Vrindavan, they can see that their lives have meaning again. They have purpose, value, support, and love.

Our pain can be a weapon, or it can be a balm. We don't get to choose what harms us. Pain is an unwelcome and unexpected guest. When the pain is fresh, it doesn't seem like we have much control over how we respond to it or how we heal from it. It feels like we lose all bodily and emotional autonomy. And for a while, that's true. We can't control our triggers or our responses to those triggers. Especially in the years immediately following a traumatic event, the nervous system adapts in ways we may not fully understand or recognize at first. We don't know how we're going to react until we do. We don't know how something is going to alter our lives until it does. Over time, though, we begin to recognize these patterns—and with that awareness, we begin to create space for new ways of responding.

Healing isn't always a straight path, and we may not even recognize it as a path while we're on it. Simply surviving, getting from one day to the next, is part of the process. There are little moments of clarity here and there when the light breaks through, and in those moments, we start to understand how our experience is shaping us. After a while, we get to the point when we can say, *Okay, here's how this is affecting me. How do I get from this point to a place where my life isn't controlled by my pain?*

Like most hard things, healing is a process. First, we have to be far enough away from the things that happened to gain self-awareness. In the immediate aftermath of a painful event, it just isn't possible to have much perspective. We're just reacting. When the fuse of a firework is lit, it doesn't stop to decide whether it wants to explode—it just does. Trauma works the same way. The nervous system reacts before we even understand what's happening. The good news is that we're not *actually* fireworks. The world isn't going to stop lighting our fuse, but we can learn how to manage the sparks differently.

Healing is a process that doesn't always feel like progress.

When I collide with my triggers, they tend to send me into anger. I lash out about ridiculous things. I slam cabinets. I say mean, cutting things. I make accusations sandwiched in between words like *always* and *never*. The story I tell myself in those moments is that I'm not safe, that everyone is against me, that no one cares about me, that I'm all alone in the world. I don't think I'm hurting anyone—I feel like everyone is hurting *me* and I'm defending myself from further harm.

Triggers can manifest themselves in all kinds of different ways. Maybe your triggers make you shut down emotionally, and you become a stoic figure moving through life. Maybe your triggers make you want to strip off all your clothes and run in the street. Triggers aren't signs of unhealed wounds; triggers are lasting reminders that we've been wounded and that our emotional chemistry has irrevocably changed.

When you get to the point when you're aware of the way your responses are causing harm to yourself or others, above anything else, approach yourself with kindness. You don't need to be ashamed or embarrassed. Your responses aren't proof that you're failing or flawed. Acknowledge your reactions and behavior without condemning yourself. Then, when you're ready, you can start exploring the changes that need to be made to gradually shift those responses.

For most of my life, my belief system asserted that if something went wrong, it was my fault. Scars of any kind were celebrated if there was a "before Jesus" and "after Jesus" associated with them. When I wrote my testimony at seventeen years old, I wrote that I'd been "clean for two years" from cigarettes. I'd smoked a grand total of maybe five cigarettes and didn't finish any of them. But I needed a good story. I needed a reason why my life had been hard before and wasn't now. *It's because I was a sinner, a smoker, and God saved me, and now I'm not a smoker and I'm also not having a hard time, glory to God.*

When I read the words of my sincere little self, I want to grab her by the shoulders, give her a good shake, like an old-school cartoon character, and tell her that she doesn't need a good testimony to be interesting or to add value to her life. But that's what my culture valued: a good story. It was the early 2000s. We loved a makeover moment. I often wonder how much pain I invited into my life because I thought I deserved it or needed it.

It's easy to look back with perspective and add a narrative that wasn't originally there. I wasn't self-aware enough at seventeen or twenty-two or twenty-six to be able to verbalize what I just described to you. I didn't know that's what I was doing, I was just trying to be a sincere follower of Christ, and I thought that's what it looked like. Pain fit neatly into two categories: the consequences of my sin or the testing of my faith. Either I was causing my pain by being distant from God or *he* was causing my pain to bring me closer to him.

Either way, scars were something to celebrate. I believed that the more I hurt, the closer I would be to righteousness. The more scars I had, the more I could be used by God to lead people to him. I surrendered, very prematurely, to a life of pain because I thought that was the right thing to do. I thought it was *good*.

My relationship to pain and how I view God's role in it changed as my theology around suffering did. I learned that God is a healer and a rescuer; he is not the author of my pain. I'd allowed the hard things I'd gone through to define me, and I lived my life going from one hard thing to the next. I was so bound by my theological framework that I couldn't see anything other than the ways I'd been harmed or how life was harder for me than it was for other people. I thought it was the life I was called to.

The ironic thing is that all the experiences I would have listed as my biggest pain points weren't what shaped my identity most. I only looked at the big events, the anno Dominis, and couldn't see how the smaller, subtler hurts had defined me. It was bad theology that made me feel small and insignificant. It was shame-filled messages that made me believe I was a bad, wicked person, even as a child. It was the mixed messaging of being handed the spiritual pressure to have an impact on the Kingdom of God while also being told that I was selfish, immature, dramatic, and too unserious for ministry.

We often don't realize how much our identity has been shaped by the things that hurt us until we begin to heal. Parenting a little girl who is just like I was as a child has helped heal a lot of those wounds for me. Getting diagnosed with ADHD as an adult has given me a new lens to view my educational and behavioral "shortcomings." Being married to someone who can't understand why I feel insecure about my appearance or my body has helped my confidence immensely. Having a best friend who celebrates even the tiniest accomplishment when she herself is the founder of a multimillion-dollar beauty company has helped me look in the mirror and say, "Yeah, you know what, I *am* that girl." And unraveling my faith and then rebuilding it has helped me embrace a faith that allows me to live freely in the love of God.

Just because there are parts of you that don't fit in a neat little Christian box doesn't make you broken. Those things about you that other people have labeled loud or quiet, blunt or withdrawn, over the top or not enough—the things that make you *you*—are not flaws. We all have parts of us that need refining, but there's no deadline on becoming. Sometimes you'll feel like you're healing up real nice, and other days you'll feel like you're right back where you started. *That's normal.* You can't bootstrap your way to a good place. Healing is a process that doesn't always feel like progress.

Healing happens slowly, in the quiet moments, until a day comes when you realize you're no longer controlled by your pain.

I teach a spiritual storytelling writing course a few times a year. The goal of the course isn't to become a good technical writer but to unpack your story, process it, and take the steps to start putting it in order so you can begin to talk about what happened to you. One of the main points I teach is that our stories are not meant for consumption.

Just because something bad happened to you and you healed from it and God carried you through it, that doesn't mean you *have* to share it. You are under no obligation, as a child of God with a good story, to use that story to bring glory to God.

We all have stories of pain and goodness. We don't *all* have to share our stories, and we don't have to share *all* our stories.

Sometimes the things that happen—and the healing that comes after—are just for you. You don't have to give your pain purpose for it to have value. You don't have to make it count. You didn't go through something awful *so that* you can help other people who are also going through something awful.

Pain serves as a map of where we've been, but it doesn't have to dictate where we go.

Pain can be a catalyst for our lives, but we aren't under any spiritual mandate to make our scars prove something. We can honor the role pain has played in shaping who we are while not feeling pressure to prevent pain for someone else or use our pain to heal theirs. God's glory is in his presence in our pain and his power in our healing. We don't prevent him from getting glory if we choose to keep our hurts private.

As we heal, the light breaks through the dark places in our heart and life, and sometimes we decide to keep parts of ourselves to ourselves to protect that light. We know there are certain hallways that will lead us back to unsafe places. Those hallways might be people who invalidate our pain or gaslight us into thinking that what happened to us isn't that bad. It might be environments that make us feel like our pain is our fault. It might be belief frameworks that tell us our healing doesn't count unless we heal the way other people think we should. It might be spiritual communities that can't accept the way our pain has transformed our beliefs about God. Knowing where those hallways are and where they lead helps protect us from entering rooms we shouldn't be in.

Choosing to protect the light isn't a weakness, nor is it a sign that we aren't actually healed. It's *wisdom.* Our scars are part of who we are, but they aren't all of us. They have shaped our life, but they don't define it. They have been our identifier, but they aren't our identity. Healing doesn't erase the scars or the impact they've had on us, but it changes the way we carry them.

Some of our scars are ones we've chosen. Some we carry against our will. And some, like the stretch of skin on my stomach that holds the scar of one loss I didn't choose and the scar of another trauma I walked into willingly, serve as a reminder of both love and loss. My grief is quieter these days, but it's still there. I'm not so acutely aware of the scars—both the ones I can see and the ones I can't—but when life brushes up against the marks of my pain, I find that I'm better equipped to take back the agency I lost in my pain.

Our pain serves as a map of where we've been, but it doesn't have to dictate where we go.

6

It's Not a Demon, It's Depression

When Deliverance Comes in the Form of a Diagnosis

MY BASEMENT, SPRINGFIELD, MASSACHUSETTS, 2021

I'M SITTING ON THE FLOOR of my basement when I finally do what my therapist (and the one before her and the one before him) has asked me to do. I'm reading the symptoms of ADHD in women.

For as long as I can remember, I've been holding a chisel in my hand, breaking myself to be better, do better. All my life, I've received and absorbed the negative statements that have been said to and about me. Particularly that I'm a liar, I'm selfish, I believe the worst about everything and see what I want to see. I can't be believed or trusted. I'm the unreliable narrator of my own life. I carry grains of salt with me and hand them out every time I tell a story.

I hate this about myself. Truthfully, I hate myself.

I glance at the website my therapist sent me. I'm side-eyeing it, holding my phone at a distance, at an angle, as if it'll explode in my hands at any moment. I cautiously read the first line, then the second, bringing the phone closer and closer, because the more I read, the less I can see. My eyes are cloudy and my face is wet.

I've seen enough. My hands are shaking. I drop the phone. I lie on the floor and pull my knees to my chest. I can't help it, I can't stop it. I'm crying from somewhere in my body I've never reached before. My sobs are loud, deep, ugly.

I'm not dying, but my life is flashing before my eyes. It's not so much scenes from my life as words that were spoken to me—words that have metabolized into my identity. *Stupid. Immature. Angry. Bitter. Irreverent. Obnoxious. Rude. Unfocused. On another planet. Dumb. Unserious.* The words are hardened clay around my body, and I feel myself breaking into pieces. I'm made of plaster, and the pieces that shatter around me are dull, dusty, cracked, and faded. I thought that was me, but it turns out I'm not made of plaster and dust; I'm made of light. I'm shining, new, illuminated by truth.

With a single diagnosis, the lies that have shaped my identity are suddenly exposed. I'm seeing myself for the first time. I'm traveling through space and time, and I discover what has always been true, but hidden.

I am not a mistake.

I am not broken.

These parts of me that I've been ashamed of are simply *Kristen*.

I feel Christ delighting around me. I haven't felt his tangible presence like this in years, but he's here and I recognize his voice. *This is what I've been trying to tell you,* I feel him say. *I have always delighted in you.* I know this moment is sacred. I know that I'm seeing myself the way he does.

I also know this moment is fleeting. I know there are people who will tell me that I'm wrong. That I am irreparably broken. That this diagnosis is wrong. They'll try to take this joy from me. They'll invalidate this sacred moment the same way they've invalidated my pain. But right now, I don't care. Right now, I know the truth, and I'm holding this moment close. Too close, maybe. But I'm afraid that if I move, it'll disappear.

Will I need a grain of salt to tell this story? I don't know. I don't care. I'm free. My God, I'm free.

My daughter is the "paying for my raising" I was promised as a kid. That's a thing old Southern people used to say. The most precocious, troublesome child is the payback for one of their parents being the source of stress for *their* parents. It's all in good fun, not the curse it sounds like—just more of a genetic inevitability.

I remember watching my cousin discipline one of her kids recently, and as he walked away, he gave me a look that his mother couldn't see. It was the same smug, mischievous look she used to give me when our parents *thought* they'd gotten us really good with their discipline, but we knew who really held the power in the relationship. I laughed and turned to my cousin and said, "You know what Papa would say about that? You're paying for your raising, girl."

There was a time when I resented being told I'd get my payback one day. I didn't *mean* to be a burden to my parents—I was just a kid! As a parent now myself, I understand these warnings weren't that serious and I wasn't really a burden, but as a kid, I just didn't get why I was due some retaliation. Was I so bad that I needed to be paid back? And I was also kind of like, *Okay, well who am I the payback for, 'cause if this is a generational thing, then one of you needs to own up . . .*

When I started to heal my body after trauma, I went to see a functional medicine doctor. He spent about ten minutes with me and said, "So, when did you get diagnosed with ADHD?" I hadn't even told him about that! I hadn't told anyone, really. He listed off all the things that made this diagnosis apparent to him, and he asked me a few more questions. He wrapped up our conversation by asking to see my fingernails.

He nodded his head and said, "So, do all the women in your family tend to be . . . *on edge*?"

All I could do was laugh. How did my fingernails expose the entire female lineage of my family?

He nodded and said, "Yeah, that's what I thought. This is genetic."

He told me that a lot of women who present the way I do and have a similar mental health history to mine tend to have variations, deletions, or malfunctions in their catecholamine-related genes. These genes regulate the production, breakdown, and function of neurotransmitters like dopamine (the one that helps you focus and feel motivated), norepinephrine (your brain's internal alarm system), and epinephrine (adrenaline, aka the fight-or-flight enabler). These chemicals are essential for things like attention, emotional regulation, cognitive function, and the body's stress response. Women with this sort of gene abnormality tend to have ADD/ADHD, anxiety, depression, and/or bipolar disorder. Without a fully functioning set of catecholamines, the body struggles to come down from a heightened state, leaving it stuck in fight-or-flight. My doctor described it as living in a constant adrenaline rush. Love that for me.

The parts of my mind that have made me feel broken come down to the wiring of my brain. My anxiety, depression, panic attacks, and the way my body responds to trauma—none of those are because I'm weaker or less spiritual than anyone else. My body just drew the short stick from the neurotransmitter pool.

Finally, I could let myself off the hook. Yet knowing all this didn't erase the years of damage that my self-hatred, emboldened by spiritual malformation, had done. It certainly didn't undo the impact my mental health struggles had on my marriage.

When I stopped treating my anxiety and depression like they were spiritual issues, I was able to get better. That's not to dismiss the power Christ has to heal, nor to deny that some people do experience miraculous healings. It's just that healing doesn't always look like the supernatural breakthrough we're taught to expect. In fact, it can hurt our faith to remain still, waiting for divine intervention, instead of seeking help in ways that are available to us. Sometimes healing comes through therapy, medication, community, or small acts of ordinary care. Sometimes it's a slow unfolding rather than a momentary display of supernatural power.

Sometimes healing is a slow unfolding rather than a momentary display of supernatural power.

And yet I know that not everyone has equitable access to those resources. Socioeconomic barriers are real. Therapy is expensive. Medication isn't always available or effective. Some people are left with little more than prayer and hope, and I'd never dismiss or diminish the faith it takes to keep believing for a miracle when support is scarce.

But I also know that if someone had told me years ago that praying away my depression wasn't the only option, that seeking help away from the altar wasn't a betrayal of my faith, I could have spared myself years of shame and suffering. So I'm writing this permission slip for you because maybe you need it as much as I did: You don't have to wait for a miracle to start healing. You're allowed to seek help in the ways that are available to you. God is just as active in the practical steps you take to heal your body and mind as he is in the miracles that don't require our participation. I would have loved a miracle. I didn't get one. But I found a way to heal, and I know you can too.

Being a Christian who struggles with mental health requires holding a complex tension. We hope that when we decide to follow Jesus, all our problems will either go away or become more manageable. He came to deliver us from darkness, and anxiety and depression are a deep, deep darkness. So if we're surrendered to Christ, we shouldn't have those in our lives . . . right? Maybe that would be true if those struggles were simply spiritual in nature, but they aren't. Chemical imbalances aren't caused by a faith that isn't surrendered or satisfied in Christ.

When I was in the deepest parts of my depression, experiencing multiple panic attacks a day, afraid to leave my house, I thought I was losing my grip. I didn't have the language to name what was happening. I didn't think it had anything to do with mental health, because those were problems *non-Christians* struggled with. They were diseases reserved for drug addicts, people with unrepentant sin, or I don't know, someone who'd gone through something really traumatic, like a *war*—or at least something a little more dramatic than crying on the kitchen floor for no apparent reason. I never would have reached for a mental health label to describe what was going on inside me. It wasn't even in the realm of possibility.

The thing about depression is that it convinces you of a lot of things that aren't true, or that are partially true, and you lose sight of reality. I didn't know anything was "wrong" with me because my depression made me feel like I had always been that way. There wasn't a "before this" in my mind. I fully believed that I'd always been this sad and would always be this sad. I believed the lies depression planted in my mind: *Everyone hates me. I'm a burden. My parents are disappointed in me. Zach is going to leave me. My kids would be better off with someone else.*

Zach didn't have a framework for understanding what was happening to me either, so he did the only thing he could think to do: He kept what was going on with me a secret. He made excuses for why I skipped church. He lied about why he was late for work or why he had to leave early. He carried my secret inside himself, thinking he was protecting us. But in reality, he was fracturing himself, me, and us. He thought I would "get past it." But I didn't. I wasn't going to.

One day I couldn't take it anymore. I'd had a panic attack that morning and begged him to come home from work. He refused. When he came home for lunch, I begged him to stay. Panic attacks are awful when they're happening, but the effects last for hours, sometimes days. It's like the aftershocks following an earthquake: The tremors don't just stop. You feel off, unsettled, sick. You can't function. I didn't feel safe to be alone, much less the only adult with our three small children. I was scared of what was happening in me and terrified of what could happen to our children. I was on the verge of psychosis but aware enough to know that I wasn't in my right mind. I begged Zach to stay, and he didn't. He barely said a word to me as he turned around, left our house, and went back to work.

When he came home at the end of the day, I said nothing. I just took the car keys, drove a few minutes down the road, and called him. My hands were shaking, my heart pounding. I wasn't sure if this would fix us or ruin us, all I knew was that I couldn't keep it in anymore. I took a breath and said, "I have something to say to you, and you're going to listen to me."

He said nothing.

"I'm *angry* at you." I had never said those words to my husband. I'd never needed to. But in the last six months of my life, I felt abandoned. I needed him, and he wasn't there. And I hated him for it.

For the next forty-five minutes, I told him everything I'd been holding inside because I was afraid that if I told him, he would leave me. I didn't care anymore. I told him that I felt betrayed by him. I was angry at him for pushing me to do things that were emotionally unsafe because he thought it would be good for me. I was angry at him for not believing my perception of things or my interpretation of circumstances because I was emotionally unstable. I was angry at him for not taking me seriously when I tried to tell him what was going on inside me. I was angry at him for dismissing me, diminishing my pain, and acting like he was ashamed of me.

That night, after our kids were in bed, we sat down in our living room and had the hardest conversation we'd ever had. I truly didn't know if we were going to stay married. Or if I even wanted to. He told me what he was thinking and feeling and experiencing, and he helped correct the narrative I had in my head about him. He apologized and made sure I knew he loved me and was trying to show it the best he knew how, but he was frustrated with me. He was being pulled in so many different directions that he couldn't fully be present anywhere. He felt like he wasn't showing up well in any of his roles, and that was beginning to chip away at his self-worth and *his* mental health.

I confessed that the reason I'd quit going to my martial arts class was because I was so angry at him that I'd started wondering what life would be like if I was married to someone else. Someone in my class. Someone who was strong and also nice to me. There wasn't a specific person—it was just the temptation that maybe there could be someone else who would take care of me the way I needed.

We both cried. We prayed together. We anointed the door-frames of every bedroom in our house with oil. We hadn't realized how dark our lives had become. We couldn't see just how much distance had grown between us until we closed it. That night, in our living room, the same one where we'd be heartbroken in a few months, the second chapter of our marriage began.

Zach stopped keeping me a secret. He finally told his mentor what was happening. His mentor responded with words that woke Zach up from a deep sleep: "You need to treat your wife like she has a terminal illness," he told him, "Because she does." He gave Zach the name of a Christian therapist and a psychiatrist.

Everything changed after that. That was the day Zach became my caretaker. I was sick, and he now felt like it was his responsibility to make sure I didn't die.

Mental health issues limit your ability to function well. When your partner doesn't have those same limitations, it's easy to feel like a burden to them. When Zach and I got married, I was hyper-independent and easy to take care of, because I didn't *want* anyone to take care of me. He was easy to take care of because he didn't need much to be happy.

As my mental health declined and his remained steady, we began to resent each other for the way things had changed, although we never said that outright. I wasn't hyperindependent anymore, but I tried to pretend I was. He wasn't as happy anymore, but he thought he was supposed to be. I felt ashamed that my needs had complicated his life, and at the same time, I was unfairly frustrated with him for not adapting as quickly as I thought he needed to.

After I started therapy, Zach began to understand the weight of what I was dealing with and how serious it was. But he understood it a little *too* deeply. It got to the point that he was afraid to leave me on my own. He wanted to always be close in case I needed him, and I hated needing him. Our relationship became about me surviving and him making it as easy as possible for me to survive. Eventually, that's all we had. There wasn't much room for anything else beyond the basics of holding it together.

We arrived at a place that was functional from a practical standpoint, but we weren't operating at optimal health. And that's okay—you don't always need to. But as my mental health improved, we realized there was something else we needed to have a good, healthy conversation about. I had to stop feeling shame about my mental health struggles. He had to stop feeling like he was (or needed to be) my hero. I had to accept that he *couldn't* be my hero, even if I wanted him to be. There's only so much one human can do for another human.

Zach needed to admit that even if he didn't see me as a burden, having a wife who wasn't always mentally well had affected him negatively. I had to accept that my husband needed therapy to process what it meant to care for me. He had to accept that caring for me was a part of the covenant he made, and that doesn't make him a hero. These acknowledgments allow us to continue to have an equal partnership. I keep him off a pedestal and accept the way my mental health has affected him. He doesn't look down on me for having mental health issues and accepts that sometimes he has to carry more weight.

No matter how I write this, it doesn't sound equitable, does it? The paragraphs always end with Zach having to be a hero but never getting to identify as one. And he can't, or our relationship will fail. He can't have the mindset that he always has to save me. And I can't have the mindset that it's his responsibility to make me happy and keep me well.

The reality is that there are inescapable, burdensome aspects of being in a relationship. When you stand in front of your person and say your vows, you only have a faint idea of what they really mean. You don't choose each other once; you choose each other over and over and over again.

A few years ago, Zach and I were going through what I like to refer to as a "fighty stage." It's one of those seasons in marriage when you don't hate each other, per se, but you're getting on each other's nerves and you don't really know why but you're just kind of like, *ugh*. You know what I mean? We finally had it out, as they say, and it went much deeper than either of us expected.

We realized that what was happening was deeply rooted in my mental health history. I was better than I'd ever been, but Zach was still nervously navigating our lives. Although my mental health hadn't been fragile in a long time, he was still moving in the same patterns as he had when things were rough. He was terrified that if he let go of the reins when it came to our house and our children, I would become overwhelmed, depressed, and a slave to my panic and anxiety again.

I sat on my bed, trying to convince him that I was okay. "What's the worst that could happen, Zach? A mental breakdown? Been there! Done that! I can do it again!" That lightened the mood, but I could still see the distress on his face, so I did what any logical, mature person would do. I flicka'd him.*

"Go on, Flicka! Leave! Get!"

Sometimes you have to bully the helpers a bit because they get *stuck*. They'll help themselves into exhaustion, and the most loving thing we can do is to set them free. Zach would stay at my beck and call every moment of every day until he literally, physically couldn't do it anymore. He would absolutely never do anything for himself, ever, if what he wanted or needed conflicted with my needs—real or perceived.

It's easy to take advantage of people like that. For Zach and me, it created emotional codependency. I needed him to take care of me to be okay, and he needed me to be okay for *him* to be okay. When I recognized how much the quality of his life hinged on me being well, I had to cut him loose.†

When the person you're married to is also your emotional safety net, that's a beautiful, wonderful thing. But eventually, you have to recognize when that dependency has become unhealthy and then change the patterns of your life to unravel that entanglement.

I didn't want my wellness to come at the expense of his joy. And vice versa. He's not my hero; he's my partner. Our covenant was not

* *flicka* (verb): A firm but loving command to gallop away like a noble stallion. Derived from the 2006 cinematic classic *Flicka*, in which a girl sets her wild horse free, because love sometimes means yelling, "Go on! Git!" through tears.

† Just in the metaphorical sense. I haven't kicked him out . . . yet.

to be rescuer and rescued but to love, honor, and cherish each other, in sickness and in health, for better or worse.

Sometimes we get so used to the sickness and the "for worse" that we don't recognize when we're in the health and "for better." The patterns we create to stay afloat in the worse can sink the ship in the better. This is when faith and trust and hope come into play in a powerful way. I have to trust that I'll be okay, even if Zach isn't immediately accessible to help with my overwhelm. I need to create systems and ways of coping that don't require Zach to rescue me. He has to trust that I'm strong and capable and that we'll be okay, even if I don't need him the way I have in the past.

We have to continue to choose each other even when what we're choosing looks different from what we expected or different from what we wanted. For better or for worse.

Telling this part of my story is stressful. Even as I'm writing a book about all the ways I've been set free from the nonsense I used to believe, I'm still fighting shame about how my mental health has affected the people I love. *Will they judge me? Am I being too honest? Will the "heroes" in the relationship feel helpless? Will the people who already feel like a burden think I'm asking them to demand more? Do I look ungrateful? Bratty? Entitled?*

I gaslight myself into thinking maybe my mental health wasn't *that* bad. Maybe I didn't need Zach as much as I thought I did. Maybe those people were right when they told me I wasn't depressed/anxious/traumatized, I was just postpartum/stressed/having a hard time. I wanted to believe them. I *so* wanted to believe them. Even after I'd accepted my medical diagnoses, I still couldn't say "I have depression" or "I'm depressed." I was shaped by the belief that I shouldn't accept things like this as part of my identity by using possessive language. So instead of saying, "I have depression," I'd say, "I struggle with sadness." I didn't have anxiety; I just got anxious sometimes. I thought if I owned those words, they would own me, so I distanced myself from them.

When we struggle with something our community has strong feelings about, we aren't in a rush to talk about it in a way that separates us from the rest of the group. We use language that's tolerable to the people around us because it's safer that way. We might acknowledge our struggle but deflect anything that would invite someone to correct us or dismiss our experience.

There's a theological panic that happens when someone who has professed faith says, "I have depression." People panic when a person's struggle doesn't fit their idea of who God is and what's promised to people who follow him. The panic often comes from a good place of wanting someone to be free from their pain, but in their desire to make sense of suffering, they offer theological platitudes that end up minimizing the person's experience.

I found a path to freedom in partnership with God, not in spite of him.

If you say, "I'm depressed" and someone responds with, "No you aren't," it destroys connection and trust. You won't be as vulnerable next time. You learn to reword your pain to make it palatable for other people. Eventually, you stop yourself from talking about it at all. How sad is it that we learn we have to lie about ourselves, even around people we should be able to trust.

We tend to have hang-ups with things we can't see and control. We like systems and formulas. We dislike it when someone challenges the order that has always made sense to us. It's uncomfortable when someone has a problem that our theology can't immediately solve. So when someone's problems can't be easily fixed with prayer, effort, or more faith, the person ends up feeling like a burden to their community. They're made to feel like if this isn't working for them, they must be the problem.

We were created to be fully integrated—mind, body, and soul. When one part is neglected, all the other parts are affected too. If one part is sick, the whole being gets sick. That's why it's not enough to throw out a spiritual prescription like "Just pray more," "Read your Bible more," or "Go talk to your pastor." Our joy and pain are both physical and spiritual. We can't compartmentalize our faith from our bodies and still expect to be well. We need wisdom to discern which paths of healing and treatment are healing and which ones might actually do harm.

When we steward our minds, we honor the one who created them. Anxiety and depression aren't proof of spiritual sickness; they're just a reality of having physical bodies. Until we see our minds as a part of our physical bodies that require physical treatment, we'll continue to strap ourselves to suffering and walk through life that way. Instead, we can treat our minds with the resources God has given us access to and experience freedom.

My anxiety and depression and PTSD weren't caused by a lack of faith, and they weren't solved by having more of it. They were caused by hormone imbalances, chemical imbalances, multiple layers of trauma, and a little bit of drawing the genetic short straw. So I got therapy for the trauma, I treated my chemical and hormonal imbalances, and I found a path to freedom in partnership with God, not in spite of him. But what really moved me from feeling shackled to the idea that this was going to be the reality for the rest of my life was locking eyes with my Creator and believing that the state of my mental health had nothing to do with my faith and was not a hindrance to it.

Unfortunately, some of the claims Christians make—often simplistic, well-intended statements—are the last thing someone internalizes before they give up. I'm so thankful this isn't my story, but I can clearly picture how my life could have gone a different way. I think that's why I get so nervous, still, when I publicly share this intimate part of my journey. I've received so many comments that made me feel hopeless. Like that my depression is a sign of discontentment. That my fears and disappointments are a sign of dissatisfaction in Christ. That wanting to hurt myself meant I was listening to demons. That I wasn't depressed, just tired. That I didn't have anxiety, I was just stressed. That all I needed to do was sleep better, eat better, pray harder, and fix my spiritual heart in every way—then I would be happy and well. It was as if they hadn't considered I'd tried all that before finally acknowledging to other people that something was wrong. The answer was simple: If I was still struggling, it was because there was something I hadn't done or thought of yet.

I'd done it all. And I was still sad.

When you open up to someone and cry for help, and they dismiss your pain because it makes *them* uncomfortable, your instinct isn't to get mad at them for their response—instead, you feel like a burden that can't be fixed. You go through a mental checklist and search your heart and find that the only logical solution is that you're broken beyond repair.

But you aren't.

One of my favorite Old Testament stories is about a man named Mephibosheth. He was the son of Jonathan, grandson of King Saul, and as a child, he had an accident that left him "crippled in both feet." This was long before the days of wheelchairs and mobility devices, so he had to be carried everywhere by servants. In ancient cultures, physical disabilities often led to exclusion and shame. But King David, described as "a man after God's own heart," did something unexpected: He actively sought Mephibosheth out, not to fix him or hide him away, but to honor him and show him kindness. David gave him a permanent place at his table, as if he were one of his own sons.[1] If David reflected the heart of God, then this story tells us something about what God's heart is like. God doesn't see us as a burden, unworthy to sit in his presence. He doesn't measure us by our usefulness. He welcomes us to his table—not in spite of our pain, but in full acknowledgement of it, just as he would any of his children.

This story is paralleled in the New Testament, when a paralyzed man's friends lowered him through a roof where Jesus was teaching. Jesus didn't chastise his friends or reject him—he healed him.[2]

Then there was the prophet Elijah, who struggled with fear and despair. Even after a dramatic victory over the prophets of Baal, he wished for death. God responded by feeding him, giving him rest, and gently encouraging him. The angel of the Lord said, "Get up and eat, or the journey will be too much for you."[3] When we are in deep exhaustion, God's response is compassion, not frustration, deprivation, or a command to pull ourselves together.

In the book of Isaiah, there's a prophecy about the Messiah that says, "He will not break a bruised reed, and he will not put out a smoldering wick."[4] This powerful imagery shows us that God is not harsh with those who are fragile. He nurtures us. Sustains us. Comforts us. Jesus confirms this truth about himself when he says,

"Come to me, all of you who are weary and burdened, and I will give you rest."[5]

I didn't know that was how I was supposed to be treated and cared for. I had no idea that kind of care was not just okay but *right*. I had to learn God's heart for the wounded by receiving that care from other people. When people who loved Jesus came into my life and held me, loved me, fed me, comforted me, and treated me with gentleness rather than harsh criticism or "bootstrap theology," not only was I able to heal, but I was also able to see God more clearly than I ever had before.

This might sound like a small thing, or even a silly thing, but one of the most significant ways I have experienced God's acceptance and care is that I don't say my name like it's a question anymore. For years, when I'd go to a coffee shop and they'd ask for a name, I'd say it like an apology.

"What's the name for the order?"

"Kristen?" As if to say, *Is that okay?* As if I was apologizing for answering their question and having the audacity to take up time and space.

Now when they ask, I state it like a fact.

"What's the name for the order?"

"Kristen." Period.

I'm not a burden. And neither are you. The people who perpetuate your feeling of being a burden are likely suffering from an acute lack of spiritual depth and understanding. They are unable to extend empathy and compassion, possibly because they never received it themselves. But after spending a lifetime considering other people's perceptions of me, wanting to make myself smaller or less so they would accept me, love me, and welcome me into their lives, I'm done. I've come to realize that even if I gain acceptance into these circles, my membership is contingent on things that are beyond my control. My worth isn't dependent on how other people value me—and neither is yours.

You aren't a burden. Not to yourself, your partner, your church, your family, or your barista. You are a magnificent being of incredible worth, created in the image of God and loved and celebrated by him. Not someday, when you have it together (whatever that means), but right now, in this moment—wherever you are, whatever you're struggling with.

> **You are loved and celebrated by God. Not someday, when you have it together, but right now—wherever you are, whatever you're struggling with.**

If there are people in your life who make you feel like your existence is an inconvenience to them, they're wrong. But if you're like me and you feel that way anyway, even without someone else saying it, I hope these words will set you free. Your needs are not a problem. Your life is not an inconvenience. The way you're wired isn't your fault.

You are not a burden.

You don't need a hero.

Your presence isn't a nuisance.

Your needs are not too much.

You have a good and kind Father who loves you and values you. He didn't come to earth to make you less of a burden. He came to share in the human experience, to feel our hurts, and to be with us in them.

7

Not Left Behind

Holy Doesn't Have to Hurt

RAYMOND JAMES STADIUM, TAMPA, FLORIDA, 2022

THE CRESCENT MOONS AND STARS ON MY DRESS catch the light as I walk into the stadium. Little girls in cowboy boots run past me while women in sparkly dresses take bracelets off their wrists and trade them with strangers. Everyone is smiling, laughing, complimenting each other on their outfits.

"Okay, you killed that fit."

"I love your boots!"

"Did you make that?"

I have never felt more welcome and included. I'm not an outlier here. I belong. I'm a part of this.

We settle into our seats and the music starts. Taylor Swift's voice echoes through the stadium as dancers with giant pieces of fabric walk onto the stage. "It's been a long time coming . . ." The crowd cheers. The anticipation builds. The energy in the room so palpable we can almost reach out and grab it, and then Taylor pops up from underneath the stage. The crowd erupts with excitement. The sound is instant and deafening, like joy has just detonated around us. The moment splits me open, and the weight I've been carrying finally pours out.

I sing until my voice goes out. I dance next to my best friend all night. I cry during the songs that I connected with during some of the most painful and confusing moments of my life. I am deep in recovery from my most recent trauma and am actively wrestling with some central aspects of my faith. But right here, in this moment, I feel like God is present in me and around me, delighting in my joy.

I don't know if I've ever felt so free to enjoy myself. I'm surrounded by people who love this music and are part of the dynamics and culture of this fandom right along with me, and I don't need to be embarrassed about it or downplay what it means to me. I don't feel silly or immature or unserious. I'm just having fun. And it feels really good to have fun.

The shift from thinking God was out to get me to believing he is actively pursuing my good was quite the shock to my spiritual nervous system. In some Christian communities, there's an assumption that holiness equals seriousness. So there's constant pressure to exercise total restraint, to never let your guard down, and to baptize every moment of joy into something spiritual. "That joke was so funny. Isn't it so sweet when saints can laugh together?" In environments like that, freedom can feel like recklessness. You learn to resist joy and fun because you're afraid of what it will cost you spiritually.

But there I was, in sequins and combat boots, feeling more spiritually grounded than I'd felt in years. Not because I was doing anything "holy," but because I was finally free, delighting in a good experience. When you believe that every decision you make dangles on a thin thread between spiritual safety and eternal damnation, every move you make feels dangerous. Living as if you're constantly in danger puts you in a state of fight-or-flight. And I know that state well.

Several years ago, I witnessed a murder when I was home alone with my children. It happened outside our living room window, and while the gunshots rang out, I sheltered my three kids under my body, away from the windows. The air was filled with screaming and screeching tires. It was horrible.*

Unsurprisingly, I was diagnosed with PTSD shortly afterward and have lived with hypervigilance ever since. I can attend fireworks shows, but hearing them in the distance while I'm home sends me into a panic. If a car backfires in our neighborhood, I am on my feet, no matter the time of day or night. I once dropped to the ground in a grocery store because a metal ladder fell.

My nervous system determines how dramatically I react, so I work hard to keep it in a calm, regulated state.† When I'm triggered, I do my best to get my body to return to neutral, because a triggered nervous system means I'm more agitated, angry, reactive, and inattentive.

Spiritual hypervigilance has a similar effect. When we view God as a judgmental king, anxious to punish and reserving grace

* I wrote more about this in my first book, *Even If He Doesn't*.

† I have five kids. Ask me how I'm doing with this. No—don't.

for only the most deserving, we live in fear, looking for his punishment around every corner. Hypervigilance gives us a false sense of security. In the thick of my battle with anxiety, I convinced myself that exploring my worst-case scenarios in vivid, descriptive ways would prepare me for if—or, in my mind, *when*—those things happened.

Our spiritual hyperawareness convinces us that staying in God's favor depends on constant self-dissection—always checking our motives, our behavior, our thoughts. We turn that scrutiny on others, using their choices as benchmarks to evaluate our own spiritual temperature. It feels safer that way. If we can keep track of everyone else's grade, we can estimate where we fall on the "good Christian" spectrum.

But hypervigilance leads to emotional exhaustion and spiritual burnout, which ultimately damages our identity. Living in constant anxiety about where we stand with God zaps all our energy. Our bodies can only take so much pressure before they break. The hyperfocus on behavior also creates strain in our relationships. We become graceless people who elevate rightness over connection and community. Paradoxically, our spiritual hyperawareness stunts our spiritual growth, because spiritual perfectionism prevents us from allowing ourselves a natural growth journey, which unavoidably involves making mistakes. When we're stuck in hypervigilance, we lose sight of other things that matter. Our focus turns primarily on ourselves—how we're performing and how other people are performing compared to us.

Hypervigilance of any kind usually stems from trauma. When a spiritual community isn't safe—emotionally, physically, or spiritually—it creates trauma in the body and brain. When spiritual leaders are abusive, passive-aggressive, overbearing, or controlling, we begin to associate that behavior with God's character. When we believe that God is more interested in what we do than how we are and who we are, we constantly live on edge, checking our behavior, making sure we're right in God's eyes. We can tell when this has gone beyond healthy self-reflection and situational awareness when we behave like we're in danger, even when we're safe.

Spiritual hypervigilance makes faith feel like survival—always scanning for threats, self-monitoring, and performing for safety. It looks like being overly sensitive to our surroundings and being on high alert for what we need to do to stay safe. It's overworking in an attempt to please God and the church, cutting off parts of our personality so we'll be absorbed into our community or family. That might mean feeling the need to say "God willing" after every statement, just in case *not* saying it causes it to not happen. Maybe we feel the need to say "It's all God" anytime someone praises us for something. Maybe we're afraid that if too many good things are happening to us, we're overdue for catastrophe. Or if something bad happens, it's always a spiritual attack.

This state of hypervigilance doesn't just impact our faith on a personal level; it shapes the way we view sin, morality, and the failures of others. When we're in a faith framework where every misstep spells catastrophe, we start to see all sin as equally dangerous, which leads to flawed thinking about forgiveness, repair, accountability, and mercy.

When posthumous sexual assault accusations were made against Ravi Zacharias, a well-known Christian apologist, the accusations were so unfathomable that many Christians had a hard time reconciling the man they loved and respected with the actions he was accused of. It opened a broader conversation about sin, temptation, and the failures of other Christian leaders. Many sermons, podcasts, and social media posts expressed a similar sentiment: "We're all one decision away from becoming Ravi Zacharias."

The accusations against Ravi Zacharias were vile. I'm a lot of things, but I'm certainly not a singular decision away from that kind of depravity. I'm not even *dozens* of decisions away from that. I understand why people say things like this—it's meant to be a reminder that none of us are immune to failure and that the compromises we make can lead us down dangerous paths. In that sense, there's wisdom in recognizing our own capacity for causing harm. But there's a difference between healthy self-awareness and living in constant fear that we are all *always* one step away from catastrophic sin. That's the kind of flawed thinking that a hypervigilant spiritual nervous system produces.

That kind of behavior doesn't just happen. It's the fruit of unexamined privilege, an abuse of power, a culture of keeping secrets, and a pattern of disregard for the humanity and value of others. To treat abuse as a single misstep isn't just naive, it's a misunderstanding of sin in general. Sin isn't just about the act, it's about what we allow to form us. When we reduce the evidence of someone's character to a single slipup, we flatten the horror of the harm and erase the responsibility of the person, the people, or the system that caused it.

If we truly believe that every Christian is always teetering on the edge of horrific harm, what does that say about our understanding of transformation, grace, and the work of the Holy Spirit?

Framing those kinds of choices as being "one decision away" creates an unnecessary fear rather than fostering the kind of spiritual formation that guards against that kind of harm.

There's no question that unchecked behavior and patterns can lead to devastating consequences—Scripture warns us about the slow erosion of character and integrity.[1] We can recognize that sin has a trajectory without assuming that every one of us is on the precipice of causing egregious harm. One mindset leads to wisdom and accountability; the other leads to paranoia and shame. "We're all one decision away" is a harmful false equivalence that fails to acknowledge the major difference between making a bad decision and sustained, deliberate mistreatment of other people. "Sin is sin," pastors teach, but the damage is not the same, and I wouldn't want to live in a world or follow a faith that asserted it is.

It's true that self-awareness and repentance are important practices in our faith. Acknowledging sin and calling it out, when appropriate, also falls within the boundaries of the practices of our faith. However, we were never meant to be sin scorekeepers, constantly searching for the things we or others do wrong so we can call them out. We were never intended to monitor ourselves and those in our community with relentless scrutiny, convinced that one wrong move could distance us from God or ruin our spiritual standing. Jesus warned against this very mindset—reminding us that the measure we use to judge others will be used against us. If we live in constant fear of spiritual failure, we inevitably project that same fear onto others.

Jesus' warning in Matthew 7 is, I think, one of the scariest things he ever said. "You will be judged by the same standard with which you judge others, and you will be measured by the same measure you use."[2] If you read that and don't automatically get to minding your own business, I don't know what to tell you.

When we become hyperfocused on behavior, we live our faith as a system of rewards and punishment. That isn't the hope of Jesus. He isn't a preschool teacher training us to sit still in class with snacks and time-outs. He is a dynamic, multifaceted God who exists in multiple forms to better lead us and love us. He created us with a human nature and intended us to be human and is well aware of the complexities our human form creates. We may not realize it, but when we build our framework of faith on the belief that God is a simple, binary God who is only capable of giving us good things for good behavior or punishing us for bad behavior, we limit who he is and what he can do. Scripture is decidedly against this kind of thinking. It defies his character. The God in Scripture is complex, nuanced, and can't be grasped. We can't understand him or his ways, which means our attempts at pinning him down to one theology, doctrine, or framework will inevitably fail because we're limiting him to our own understanding.

We act like we have to chase after God's goodness when Scripture says his goodness is chasing after *us.*

Our need for answers is as old as God's breath in our human bodies. Adam and Eve wanted to know, so they ate. They knew in part—and that's all any of us will ever know. Never the whole, just the parts. And yet we still search for the code to unlock God's blessing or to protect us from his punishment. We search for meaning in our suffering: "God must be teaching me something." We look for signs of his confirmation and seek to hear his voice. We sing the words "You give and take away," and we live as if God dangles his goodness like a carrot in front of us. We act like we have to chase after his goodness when Scripture says his goodness is chasing after *us*.

If we believe that God is withholding his blessing and favor until we prove ourselves through our good behavior, then we'll live like nothing is safe and internalize the message *I'm not safe with God*. Neither are our children and our families or anyone else we love, because God can take them. Neither is our house, because God can take that. And neither is our safety, because God can take that too. Some might say this is living by faith—trusting that we'll be okay no matter what, even if those things happen. And I think there's truth to that. But there's a difference between having faith that we'll be okay if these things happen and living our life as if God can and will impulsively take the things we love at any moment.

We crave certainty, so we try to fit faith into neat categories: Good things happen to good people, bad things happen to bad people. But Scripture shows us that God doesn't operate within the boundaries of our human binaries. He is both protector and nurturer, both just and merciful. When we let go of rigid frameworks, we can step into a fuller experience of his goodness—goodness that is based on trust, not fear.

Sometimes it's easier to believe that God wants to punish us and teach us than it is to believe that he wants what's good for us. If we believe our primary identity is as sinners in the hands of an angry, punitive God, we'll live like scared children, flinching in the presence of a volatile parent—always watching, never resting. But if we believe that we're loved and cherished by God and that he desires *good* for us, we'll live like we're free—because we are.

My mom always called my dad a pessimist, and he would always respond, "I'm not a pessimist—I'm a realist! I just see things the way they are." I inherited that trait from my dad, but I can admit what my dad won't: I'm actually a pessimist. Well, a reformed pessimist now.

I don't think it's entirely my fault that I lean toward the negative. When I was a kid, I was fully convinced I was psychic. I thought I had powers, but I didn't tell anyone because, you know, well, *witchcraft* and all that. But I would look at a person or a situation, and I could see in my head what was going to happen in the future. Then those things would happen. Now that I think about it, the flashes Raven would have in *That's So Raven* are pretty accurate to my experience, but stick with me here. I wasn't dabbling in sorcery. Turns out, it was something I didn't have a name for at the time that I later discovered is *pattern recognition*. I couldn't actually see the future; my brain was just subconsciously ordering things into patterns. My "predictions" were just the ability to recognize connections and anticipate consequences that were likely to happen again.

But for most of my life, I just thought I had powers.

On the heels of multiple traumas, my "realism" became chronic pessimism. When something bad happened to my family, my response was, "Well, yeah, of course that happened—that's the pattern of my life." I resigned myself to a life of suffering. I believed nothing good was coming for me. I was just holding my breath in between the bad things.

At one point, I was pretty sure I knew the calendar pattern for my traumas. They always happened in March or May. Always. If they've happened in March or May in the past, they'll always happen then, so every spring, I braced myself for hard things. I lived under the weight of a faith defined by fear. Every decision felt like a potential spiritual catastrophe; every blessing came with an undercurrent of suspicion.

But what if this isn't the way God intends us to live? What if, instead of believing that God was waiting to test or punish us, we could believe he is conspiring for our good?

For me, this shift didn't happen overnight, but it started with a little etymology.

One day I came across a word I'd never heard before: *pronoia*, the belief that the universe is conspiring for your good. It's essentially the opposite of paranoia. Instead of assuming that harm is inevitable, pronoia assumes that goodness is inevitable. I read about it and thought, *Huh. Must be nice.*

To be clear, both are psychological delusions. So let's not rush to romanticize the one with better branding. However, something in me wouldn't let go of this idea. What if I just tried it? What if I lived as if good things instead of bad things were chasing after me? I grabbed my journal and wrote:

> What if, instead of believing that God is always out to get me or teach me a lesson, I believed that he is conspiring for my good?

That thought felt revolutionary. And strangely . . . familiar. I flipped through my Bible and found the verse that echoed it almost exactly:

> Surely goodness and mercy shall follow me all the days of my life.[3]

Goodness and mercy weren't just randomly appearing in my life. They were *pursuing* me. They were following me. God didn't say punishment was pursuing me. Or hardship. Or some divine test of endurance. *Goodness.*

That realization shifted something in me. When something bad happened, instead of immediately thinking, *Of course this happened—this is just my life*, I took a breath and thought, *It's going to be okay. God is conspiring for my good, not for my harm.*

But what does *good* mean? If we don't know what God's goodness looks like, we won't recognize it even when it's on our heels.

When we think about what *good* means, we often assume it looks like ease. Our Western idea of *good* is a pain-free, healthy, financially blessed life. What we see as God's goodness usually looks a lot like what *we* want and desire. But if we can't pick up our idea of what *good* means and drop it into any culture, any country, any era, and any circumstance and have it look the same, it isn't God's goodness. Is he still good for someone in poverty? For someone with an incurable disease? For someone who loses a child? For someone struggling with their mental health? For someone whose spouse cheats on them? For someone who doesn't have access to clean water?

God is conspiring for your good, not your harm.

God's goodness isn't defined by our physical prosperity. God isn't conspiring to give us an easy ride. (I wish, though.) His goodness is his presence, his mercy, his grace, his kindness. It's what gives us comfort in suffering and disappointment and peace when life is unraveling around us. His goodness isn't a transaction that he gives in exchange for our good works. And it isn't always big and bright or miraculous.

When we know what his goodness looks like, we'll start noticing the ways it's already present in our lives—ways we might have overlooked when we were busy bracing for impact. We'll see it in the unexpected kindness of a stranger or a friend, the way sunlight hits the kitchen table, the way laughter bursts from inside, even on heavy days.

Over time, my chronic pessimism (sorry, Dad—my *realism*) began to fade. It took work to unlearn the deeply ingrained belief that God's goodness is something I had to earn or something fragile that could be taken away at any moment. But once I started looking for his goodness, his presence, I realized it had been there all along.

What an audacious thing to believe—that the God of everything, who created everything, who is in everything, who can do anything, who is all-powerful and all-knowing, would want good things for us. The Bible says God wants us to live abundantly, to have joy, to have the desires of our hearts, to have delight.[4] The Americanized prosperity gospel version of that says God wants us to be rich, to not have problems, to never be sick or sad or broken. But that bastardizes the sacred, beautiful texts that point to a God who sources our abundance with himself, not our circumstances.

It isn't the absence of bad things (or the presence of tangible prosperity) that gives us good; it's the fullness of *him*.

C. S. Lewis wrote a line in The Chronicles of Narnia that describes the paradox of God's character. The Pevensie children have heard about Aslan, and they find out he is a lion. "Ooh," Susan says, "I'd thought he was a man. Is he—quite safe?"

Mr. Beaver responds, "Safe? . . . Who said anything about safe? 'Course he isn't safe. But he's good. He's the King, I tell you."[5]

If you read the books, you'll find that Aslan *is* quite safe in the sense that he's bold, he's brave, he's a protector. He has all the characteristics of a fearsome lion and all the gentleness and goodness of a loving King. The only creatures that aren't safe around Aslan are the ones that use their power to harm others.

This imagery of God as a lion is used over and over again in Scripture as a way to characterize what seems like his dichotomous nature. Scripture describes God through a variety of metaphors—some powerful and fearsome, others tender and nurturing. But we often emphasize only one aspect of his nature, and when we do that, we limit our understanding of who he truly is. God is both protector and comforter, both fierce and gentle. We need to grasp both aspects to get a full picture of his love.

God is described as a protector: a lion, a fortress, a shield, mountains that protect a city, a gate that keeps out predators, a hedge, a rock, a strong tower. And he's described as a nurturer: a mother eagle, a hen gathering her chicks, a comforting mother, a nursing mother, a midwife, a mother bear.[6]

Some struggle with the idea that God is fierce because it can make him seem distant or even threatening, especially to those with trauma tied to authoritarian figures. Others struggle to embrace the idea that God is tender because they think that makes him seem weak. But does being like a lion mean God is *only* a protector? Does being like a mother mean God is *only* tender? If humans are multifaceted creatures, surely God is even more so.

If you grew up in an environment that was verbally abusive under the guise of "strong leadership" or had what psychologists refer to as an "eggshell parent,"[7] the image of God as a lion might feel threatening, not comforting. If you grew up with a militant authority figure in your life who made you feel unsafe and caused harm to your identity and your nervous system, God will not seem safe to you if he's presented that way. There's no safety in a God who looks and sounds like people who harmed you.

If you've never experienced the nurture of a parent, it might feel unsafe to think of God in that way. It might even be triggering. Maybe nurture doesn't feel safe to you because you learned that it's only given under certain conditions and can be withdrawn at any time. Maybe you grew up with confusing messages of love and affection, and you struggle to know what's appropriate because the adults in your life harmed you in some way. If you feel safer when people are at a distance, you'll feel safer when you keep God at a distance as well. You might tell yourself you don't need his love in that way. You're self-fulfilled and self-sufficient. It's better for God to be a general in the army or a distant king, ruling over your life but not present in it. You accept his love, as long as it comes with the strong hand of a good, honorable leader. When love doesn't feel safe, a God of love won't feel safe either.

God is a fortress and strong tower, and he is a loving mother with a baby at her breast. He is a lion, and he is a hen.

The problem with all this is that when we lean too heavily on a singular aspect of God's character, we deny ourselves from knowing him fully. To only see him as a warrior is to miss his gentleness. To only see him as a comforter is to miss his power. He is a fortress and strong tower, and he is a loving mother with a baby at her breast. He is a lion, and he is a hen. He is a midwife, and he is a mountain. If we only trust his wrath, we become wrathful. If we only trust his nurture, we become vulnerable to predators. God is *both*, he is *all*, he is so much more. We are safest when we embrace the fullness of who he is.

There's tension in understanding who God is and who he is to *us*. We insist on the images of God that feel truer to us. We hold tightly to the metaphors that make sense to us (and that feel safe to us) and dismiss the ones that leave us feeling out of control and unstable. But when we minimize an aspect of God's nature, we idolize our *concept* of God rather than who he has revealed himself to be. The revelation of God through Scripture, nature, conscience, prophets, poets, historians, and Jesus Christ himself is a rich and colorful tapestry. If we cut off a corner, we'll never see the full beauty of the intricacies God has woven together and revealed to us.

God's love is not weak or enabling.

His justice does not seek harm.

His power does not assert control.

His love doesn't weaken theology.

His strength protects us.

His love heals, comforts, and guides us.

When we embrace the full character and nature of God, our faith is emboldened and empowered. A safe, loving home requires both nurture and strength. And when our home is safe and loving, we want to invite our friends over! Faith works the same way.

When we misunderstand God's character, we also misunderstand what he desires for us. Some traditions overemphasize his abundance, treating faith like a formula for material wealth. Others insist that self-denial and suffering are the only paths to holiness. But if God is both a fierce protector and a nurturing provider, then wouldn't his vision for our lives include both discipline and delight?

My husband and I met at Bible college. I was fresh out of a two-year relationship; he had just made a vow to God to not date for a year. We crashed into each other's best-laid plans and, despite our best efforts, fell in love. Zach, bless his heart, panicked immediately. He liked me *too* much. He wanted to spend *too* much time with me.

He had started following Jesus in high school, at the height of the youth culture that gave us *Acquire the Fire*, *Jesus Freaks*, and *I Kissed Dating Goodbye*. Christian teenagers would go on elaborate mission trips inspired by early missionaries who would pack their belongings in coffins, expecting to never come home. As teenagers, we were presented with the hardest, most challenging version of Christianity and were promised eternal life for it. The message was simple: Lay down your life, be willing to die, stay away from the opposite sex.

I had dissected and filtered out a good bit of that already, so by the time we met, I was something of a chaotic riot. I was funny, loud, always looking for an adventure, always doing something stupid to make someone laugh. I wanted to hang out with him all the time, and I didn't, for even a second, think of it as a distraction from what we were at college to do or learn. Zach did, though. When things got too chummy, he disappeared.

For the first six months of our relationship, I never knew which version of him I would get. Were we friends today? Dating? Classmates who didn't acknowledge each other at all? He was all in, and then just as fast, he'd be all out. He was also, at one point, only partially out, because he thought maybe God brought him to Ohio to do a summer internship to meet his future wife (which was not me, by the way, because I was doing *my* internship in Paraguay. That was a fun email).

In Zach's mind, God didn't want him to have delights. If he enjoyed anything, it needed to be sacrificed, and that included our relationship. His God was impossible to please. He loved God so genuinely and wanted to do everything right. He tried to learn all the rules so he could follow them exactly and hear God say, "This is my beloved son, with whom I am well-pleased." I was probably the distraction Satan was using to distract Zach from his calling. Nothing was more terrifying to him than displeasing God and missing what he'd been called to do.

Zach's struggle wasn't unique—many of us were conditioned to believe that anything we loved, apart from God himself, was a distraction from our commitment to him. We were taught that enjoyment and spiritual maturity couldn't coexist, that we must always sacrifice something to prove our devotion. But Scripture tells a different story. Again and again, God invites us into joy, abundance, and delight—not as a test, but as a reflection of his own generous nature.

Zach did, eventually, unlearn this theology and realize that I was the best thing to ever happen to him—no packing our things in coffins required. But that ascetic framework isn't easy to let go of. It creates chronic stress for simply living a normal life. It makes us feel like we have to overspiritualize our joy. We feel the need to baptize everything we enjoy: "This coffee is so good. Glory to God!" Or we justify things we want to do by giving them a spiritual purpose: "I'm buying this new dress because I was invited to a party and I want to be the best example of Christ by dressing with excellence." Or "I want to be rich—but only because the more money I have, the more I can give!" Our need to redeem everything is rooted in an ascetic form of faith that makes us believe we can't enjoy something just to enjoy it or desire something just to desire it. If joy doesn't have a godly goal, we see it as self-indulgent—and therefore, it must be *bad*.

When everything fits into neat little categories, especially if there are only two categories, we can make sense of the world. We can have control (or at least, we think we can). But faith and control don't coexist very well, do they? If I can control the world around me, I don't need faith. If I can see the walls around me and the steps in front of me, and I know exactly what God wants and exactly the right choice in every situation, then I don't need the Holy Spirit. I just need to do the math. But when we live our life inside the confines of what feels like a sure thing, we might miss out on the abundance God longs for us to have.

We add a lot to God's Word when we create all these caveats. We add *Yeah, buts* to things that are directly from the written revelation of God.

God "richly provides us with everything for our enjoyment" (1 Timothy 6:17, NIV).
Yeah, but . . . enjoyment must result in worship, and enjoying worldly things won't lead us to worship our Creator.

"That each of them may eat and drink, and find satisfaction in all their toil—this is the gift of God" (Ecclesiastes 3:13, NIV).
Yeah, but . . . the gift of God is eternal life. This verse is about eternal satisfaction, not an earthly one.

Jesus says, "If you, then, though you are evil, know how to give good gifts to your children, how much more will your Father in heaven give good gifts to those who ask him!" (Matthew 7:11, NIV).

Yeah, but . . . God determines what's good, not us. To us, sometimes "good" looks like pain and suffering and loss. So sometimes "good" hurts.

Oof. It's exhausting, isn't it? If the revelation of God in Scripture isn't enough to convince us that God wants us to enjoy the life he's created for us, look outside! The created world is not simply functional; it's *beautiful.* There's no reason for so many different species of daisies. Surely the white ones would do the trick. What about birds? Why so many? What about lakes and oceans and ponds and meadows? Surely if they were just functional, they would all look the same. Our created world is both beautiful and functional, soft and hard, tall and deep, dense and shallow. There is still land on earth that has not been explored. The oceans remain a mystery. The greater universe will probably never be known. God is an artist who took great pleasure in creating our world and our bodies. A celebration of the creation is a celebration of the Creator.

How could a God who created so much to be enjoyed require that we enjoy it with restrictions? All good gifts come from him, so all things we enjoy point to him. He is good, and he called his creation good, and he calls *us* good. It's only reasonable to believe that a God from whom good overflows would also want good to overflow in our lives as well.

So what happens when we stop seeing God as a cosmic judge and start embracing him as the giver of good things? How does our faith shift when we stop bracing for disaster and start trusting in abundance?

For me, it meant reshaping the way I saw everything—from my past wounds to my present joy. It meant replacing fear with freedom and scarcity with trust. And it meant living with a new set of beliefs—ones that changed everything about how I moved through the world.

When we believe that God is out for our good and not for our harm, our lives begin to mold around these beliefs:

- Goodness and mercy are following me, chasing after me—every day, for all my life.
- God isn't out to get me.
- God wants good things for me.
- God wants me to live abundantly.
- God wants me to have joy.
- God wants me to have desires (and those desires don't have to be only for spiritual things).
- My delight is not a sin.
- God delights in me.

What would happen if you believed that God was both safe and good? What if you truly believed and embodied the idea that God is conspiring for your good? Like a mother planning a magical Christmas morning, or a long-distance boyfriend turning off his location and secretly texting all his girlfriend's best friends so he can surprise her for her birthday, God is joyfully conspiring for your good. Not to get you, not to teach you, not to harm you, not to bargain with you, not to reward you—just because he loves you.

This is the antidote to spiritual anxiety and hypervigilance: to embrace the idea that God is both protector and pursuer of our goodness. When we accept this reality, it transforms how we live and how we embody our faith. We can face life's challenges with openness and hope because we know that God is our defender *and* our comforter. We can celebrate our abundance with abandon because God is the giver of good things and our hope in the midst of our lack. The more we seek the true character of God, the more we'll understand him and the more colorful our picture of God will become.

For so many of us, faith has never felt like freedom—it has felt like restriction, fear, a means to an end. We've spent years fearing rejection, bracing for loss, trying to earn what was meant as a gift, instead of resting in the love of God and our community. But the invitation God gives to all of us has never been to live anxious, with our shoulders tight, hiding and hating who we are. He invites us to himself—to be fully known and fully loved without fear.

The work of healing is not just to unlearn all the malformations of faith but to relearn what it means to truly live.

8

I Kissed Hating Myself Goodbye

Ending the Animosity Between You and the Body You Live In

NATHAN BILL PARK, SPRINGFIELD, MASSACHUSETTS, 2024

MY FEET ARE SLAPPING THE PAVEMENT, one after the other. I can feel the rhythm of my sneakers on the sidewalk, sending vibrations through my calves and straight to my racing heart. I try to time my pace to the beat of the music in my ears. Griff is singing. "I miss staring at the ceiling 'cause it felt so tall / I miss sleeping to the sound of the kids next door, I do / I miss me, I miss me too." Tears are streaming down my face. This is holy. This is church.

I meet with God on these sidewalks, in this playlist. I miss me too. I miss me too. I wonder if I've even met me. I'm a stranger to myself, settling into myself. I feel like I'm on the cusp of something. A metamorphosis, maybe. I miss me. I'm finding me. I'm becoming me.

I don't know if a runner's high has anything to do with this, but every step feels like I'm running straight into the arms of God. I envision him ahead of me with open arms, celebrating the movement of my body and the resilience of my mind. I feel him next to me, running alongside me, whispering things that are true about who I am. I don't feel broken anymore. I feel strong. I feel like I'm running to myself.

I think that at the end of this run, I'll collide into the version of me I've always been—one that's been hidden by my trauma, my self-hatred, the lies I've believed about myself. I'm proud of how my body has carried me. I'm grateful for the ways I'm able to move and stretch and run. I'm acutely aware of how my mind has limited my physicality, and I'm drunk on the joy of feeling at home in my body at last.

I pick up the pace as Griff sings the last chorus. I missed me too. But I think I'm home now.

So, I'm a runner now. And I can almost guarantee no one else, in all of history, has become a runner the way I did. The thing is that I speak in metaphor. A lot. This particular time I spoke in metaphor led to me being forced to train for a 5K, and that's the most amount of trouble I've gotten into trying to write prolifically. It's a hazard I wasn't aware of.

What happened is that I posted on social media about finally feeling like I was coming out of survival mode and waking up to my life and how I was excited to be a person again and get things done, put my hard pants on, and really just . . . take life by the horns, you know? But I didn't say all that. What I did say was "I'm ready to run!"

The next day, I got a text from a new friend. "I saw your post! I want to run with you!"

To be clear—I thought we were speaking in metaphor. "Okay! Let's go!" I responded, because in my head, this meant we were going to "run at life" together. We were going to wake up early and get our houses in order and get projects done and—I don't know, it was metaphorical, okay?

She responded, "Okay, but I'm a slow runner!"

And I'm an idiot, because I thought she meant she has a lot going on in her life and isn't ready for an intense go-get-'em type of run at life.

"Oh, don't worry, my run is more like a brisk walk." Meaning, *I'm with ya, girl. No pressure here. We can only do what we can do.*

And then she sent the text that made me say out loud, "Oh noooo . . ."

"Okay, I'm fully committed now! Just ordered some running gear!"

Shoot. Shoot. Shoot. Shoot.

I thought we were doing a bit—I didn't know I was committing to physical activity! This had gone too far. I couldn't tell her it was a metaphor now that she was financially invested in the situation. I did what any reasonable, mature person would do. I texted her back and said, "I'm so sorry—that was a miscommunication. I was speaking metaphorically. I have no intention to actually run."

Yeah, that's not what happened. That wouldn't be much of a story, would it?

What I *did* say was "Yay! When do you want to run together?"

Why didn't I tell her the truth? I don't know—ask my therapist—but I bought sneakers the next day and I've never looked back. My life got significantly better the moment my feet hit the pavement, and I've never been more grateful for a metaphor gone awry.

I never did tell her, by the way. I had this image in my mind of crossing the finish line of our 5K, turning to her, and saying, "It was a metaphor!" But we never actually took up running together and it never came up again. I guess she'll find out when she reads this book. Great. Well. The gig is up. Sorry, Rachel. Or, I guess, thank you?

I've never felt fully at home in my body. It's fair to say my relationship to it has been one of near-constant contention. I've always moved through the world awkwardly—bumping into things and people, collecting mysterious bruises I can never account for. I lack the spatial awareness and grace of my mother, whose every step is calculated, intentional, precise. Why can't I be like that?

I am the last Southern-born woman in a long line of Southern-born women who never let a hair fall out of place or allowed a word to escape their lips out of turn. I didn't get that coding in my genetic makeup. I fumble through life, speaking before I think and laughing too loudly at things that aren't supposed to be funny. If "out of turn" was a person . . . know what I mean?

But my discomfort in my own body was more than just clumsiness; it was a deep sense of detachment that eventually grew into resentment toward the physical form I was born into. Why couldn't I be naturally beautiful? If I was pretty, maybe it would make up for how much space my clumsy personality took up in a room. Maybe I'd be pretty if I was smaller.

I was eighteen years old the first time I decided not to eat. It started with the slow unraveling of a two-year relationship. He was already pulling away, his attention shifting to a coworker who was conveniently not a fourteen-hour drive away. I knew the relationship wasn't right for me, but before I accepted the reality of that, I tried to attract his attention by making myself smaller. I thought I could make myself so fragile that he'd want to rescue me.

I was already small when this started. But I wanted to be smaller, so I ate saltine crackers and sucked on marshmallows to curb my appetite. No one really noticed my weight dropping, but I did. I liked the way my collarbones stuck out from my shirt. I liked the curve of my hip bones against my low-rise jeans. I liked when people hugged me and said, "I feel like I'm gonna break you!" I liked when people asked me to climb into small spaces to retrieve something because I was the only one small enough to fit. I lived for the praise of my frailty.

I ended up breaking up with the boy, but my addiction to controlling the way my body looked stayed. I didn't tell anyone. I didn't think about what I was doing as an eating disorder or "disordered eating." It was just something I did. I cut out pictures of celebrities whose bodies I admired, unaware that they were struggling with addictions or eating disorders. I pasted their images in my journal and called it "inspiration." I wanted my ribs to be visible like theirs. I wanted my fingers to look long and thin wrapped around a Starbucks cup. I wanted clothes to drape over my body the same way.

I've never liked the presence of pain medication in my body because my body *really* likes pain medication. I've stopped morphine drips during painful medical procedures because while I like the way certain medications make me feel like I'm floating above my body, I have a visceral reaction against that enjoyment. There's something instinctual in me that flags the danger of an addictive feeling. That's exactly what happened with my controlled and disordered eating. There wasn't a singular moment when I knew I needed to stop; it was the gradual realization that I was enjoying something I could get addicted to (or already was).

I started eating more at each meal. Still, I didn't tell anyone, because I didn't think there was anything to tell. I didn't consider it a big deal. Until one night, my future sister-in-law and her friend were sitting in my dorm room. I casually said, "Hey I ate a whole meal today. Finished it and everything."

They looked at me kind of sideways and said, "What do you mean? Why aren't you eating whole meals every day?"

Their furrowed eyebrows and glances at each other showed me what I hadn't been able to see when I looked in the mirror. What I'd been doing wasn't benign. "Kristen, if you don't tell someone, we will."

So I did.

My resident director (who was also a nurse) put me on a nutrition plan. She wanted me to check in weekly and eat a banana every day. "They'll make your boobs grow," she told me with a wink. So I ate a banana every day, and I was probably just gaining weight, but the word got out about the bananas. A few weeks later, Zach and his friends sat down at my table for breakfast, griping about the sudden banana shortage in the cafeteria.

I always want to tie up a story like that with a bow, as if identity and self-hatred can easily be solved by going up a cup size. But that's not when I healed—that was just when I recognized the wound. Part of the reason it took me so long to see the truth about my disordered eating is because of how I'd been taught to think of bodies and brains. Evangelicalism often separates the body from the mind. Sure, the body needs medicine and food and exercise, but the mind only needs faith. The theology of "flesh vs. spirit" creates a false divide between what can be seen (the body) and what cannot (the mind). In this framework, the mind can be overcome in ways that the body cannot. That misinterpretation has created so much harm. It's left so many of us suffering in silence, ashamed of our symptoms, begging for relief at the altar, unsure if we're even allowed to ask for help.

My struggle with my body has never been about my body or food—it's about worth. I didn't have the words or understanding to articulate this at the time, but now I can see how much of my perception and beliefs about my body, my mind, and my worth were malformed by my theology.

Evangelical Christianity teaches that we are born into a broken world, incapable of being good but for the presence of Christ in our lives. Some traditions teach that we enter the world actively sinning. Others say we simply have the *propensity* toward sin and that at some ambiguous "age of accountability,"* we cross over from innocent to guilty by default. Either way, the message is the same: You're broken. Your default setting is bad.

I grew up with the age of accountability theology. I didn't know that this wasn't *anywhere* in the Bible—written or implied—until I was much older than I'd like to admit. And while there has never

* The "age of accountability" has no firm basis in Scripture or early church tradition, but it gained traction in evangelicalism—especially during the Billy Graham era—as a theological work-around. As evangelicals moved away from infant baptism (which some saw as a way of cleansing original sin), they faced a dilemma: If children are born sinful but baptism is symbolic, what covers a child who dies young? Rather than reexamining doctrines of original sin and salvation, the idea of an age of accountability was introduced to plug that theological hole. Though verses like Deuteronomy 1:39; Isaiah 7:16; and Romans 2:14-15 are sometimes cited, the concept is not explicitly taught in the Bible. See Millard J. Erickson, *Christian Theology*, 3rd ed. (Baker Academic, 2013), 581.

been a consensus on when we cross the threshold into "Now you're old enough to be responsible for your sin before God," I took sin very seriously. By the time I was eleven years old, I fully identified as a sinner and lived my life in such a way as to avoid hell at all costs. If someone called me a brat, I believed them. If they called me selfish, I believed them. And why wouldn't I? If your theology teaches you that your nature is "bad and broken," then isn't every flaw or mistake just a confirmation of that?

For some of us, that theology drives us toward striving, trying to prove that we are holy enough, disciplined enough, refined enough to overcome our brokenness. For others, it leads to a sort of resignation. We give up on goodness because we know we're incapable of it. For a lot of us (and this was true for me), it led to something else entirely: self-hatred disguised as sanctification.

Sanctification is often taught as a linear journey—the closer we get to Jesus, the more refined and holy we'll be. It's presented as the chipping away of the old and baptizing into the new, with the goal of becoming more and more like Christ until we achieve ultimate holiness in death. But this view assumes that transformation is always upward rather than messy, cyclical, and deeply human. In practice, sanctification often looks less like perfection and more like learning to stay (imperfectly, but faithfully) near to God.

I believed that if I could just fix myself—be smaller, quieter, holier, more disciplined—then I'd become worthy. I thought if I could break myself down and rebuild without all the garbage, I could make something lovable out of what was, by nature, unlovable. I thought that's what God wanted from me.

The problem is that (1) we can't sanctify ourselves and (2) we can't escape the hardwiring of our brains. And we don't need to. When we conflate neurological wirings with sinful nature, we burden people with shame over things that aren't moral failings, just differences in the way they engage with the world. That kind of weight doesn't lead to greater holiness—it leads to misery for those whose brains are off the spectrum of "typical." Beyond the personal toll, it shapes our communities into places of quiet (or not so quiet) judgment rather than belonging—especially for the neurodivergent, those with disabilities, and those with personalities that don't match the social or emotional norms often mistaken for spiritual virtue.

If your church teaches that anxiety is a result of a lack of trust in God because "God has not called us to live in fear," you'll believe that the solution to your anxiety is to have more faith. If you try to have more faith and the anxiety persists, you'll believe that the problem is your faith.

What if you struggle with depression and your pastor preaches a sermon about how Christ offers a constant source of joy? If he teaches that "rejoice always" means we never have a reason to lack joy, you'll come to the conclusion that depression isn't compatible with the Christian walk. So if you're depressed, something's wrong with you.

If you've experienced trauma, the message "Through him, I've overcome all things" might make you feel defeated because your trauma still feels like it could very well overcome you. If you don't feel like an overcomer, that message might make you feel weak or like Christ has abandoned you.

Sometimes the promises of God feel like they're only for people whose bodies and brains work better than ours do. Those theologies shape our experiences and leave us feeling like we're doing something wrong or there's something wrong with us if we can't get over whatever we're struggling with.

Shortly before I was diagnosed with a panic disorder, I scribbled these words in my journal:

> I have so many fears. Unnecessary and controlling fears. I know they are not from you. I know that they are flesh-y and that they are born from lies. My need for control feeds them and my lack of trust in you gives them space to grow. Forgive me. Please forgive me. I hate that I am this way. It feels like it will never stop, but I know that you're my healer, and I am bravely asking you to heal me. Heal my mind, my heart. Whatever is broken in me right now, heal it. I know that you can and that you will.

He didn't. My panic attacks weren't caused by a lack of control over my thoughts or a lack of trust or anything spiritual at all. They were a physiological response to several things happening in my life. Having a baby, moving across the country, and being in an unstable, high-stress church environment sent my body into chaos.

The reason I was in the ER every week, hooked up to EKG machines, fighting with nurses who wouldn't believe me that I was having a heart attack,* wasn't because I didn't trust God enough. I was there because I was struggling, alone, and unsupported by

* I wasn't.

my community. God didn't heal me in the supernatural way I was begging him to, and I didn't fix myself in the way I'd been taught to. In fact, it took years, several more traumatic events, a terrifying season of depression, and a few mental breakdowns before I finally found freedom and healing from a life plagued by poor mental health and emotional dysregulation.

That freedom wasn't waiting for me on the pages of Scripture or at the altar, although I wish it had been that simple. The Bible doesn't talk specifically about panic attacks or provide a blueprint for curing depression or trauma-induced dysregulation. There's no verse that says, "When your nervous system is fried from chronic stress, seek therapy, medication, and rest." But Scripture does teach us about the compassion of Christ for the hurting. It displays the character of God in his kindness toward those who are afraid, wounded, and in need of rest. He didn't say, "Just put your hard pants on and trust me!" He never demands our grit or requires us to power through our pain. Just like he did for Elijah, God sees when the journey is too much for us and tells us to wait, rest, and eat.[1]

God calls his children into wholeness, and he provides a way to live into that wholeness.

God calls his children into wholeness, and he provides a way to live into that wholeness. He gives us wisdom and discernment and community. He meets us with love and mercy on the way to wholeness—whether that's with a therapist, in a support group, in a psych ward, at the altar, on the floor of your bedroom, or at the pharmacy. Seeking a path forward, whatever that looks like, is an act of faith. It takes a lot of courage to say, "I need help, and even if this isn't how I was taught to get it, I know that God is with me."

Shortly after my thirty-fourth birthday, I got my last official diagnosis, the final Pokémon. *Congratulations, Kristen—you have ADHD, inattentive type.*

The process for getting a diagnosis isn't easy. Although some people swear that doctors are just handing out ADHD labels these days, it's simply not true. Laughably false, actually. Women, in particular, have a much harder time getting diagnosed because, well, women tend to be *believed* a lot less, but also because ADHD presents differently in women than men. Every woman in my life who has been formally diagnosed has had to go through multiple therapists and fight for her diagnosis so she can get the help and support she needs.

My story is a little different. In my case, my therapists weren't the ones refusing a diagnosis—I was. For years. Over a span of eight years, three different therapists encouraged me to go through the process of getting diagnosed. Do you know how severe your ADHD must be to have multiple therapists, at different offices, trying to convince *you* of it? Stage 4, my friends.

I laughed at the first therapist. I rolled my eyes at the second. By the time the third one brought it up, unprompted and unprovoked, I thought maybe there might be something to it. After I finally got the diagnosis, not only did my past make sense, but my present reality became a whole lot brighter. If I had ADHD, that meant my mind wasn't broken. I wasn't selfish. I wasn't a bad kid. I wasn't incapable. I wasn't worse than anyone else. My brain just worked a little differently.

I'd spent my life trying to use prayer and spiritual practices to change my behavior and thought process, but what if it was simpler than that? What if the solution wasn't "pray and wait"? What if there were tangible things I could do and medications I could take and practices I could incorporate into my life? What if I didn't need a supernatural miracle?

Turns out, I didn't.

I needed supplements, medication, understanding, and knowledge. I read books, listened to podcasts, and started to take care of my body in a way that improved my focus and attention. In the same way that figuring out your learning style can help you retain information better in school, learning that I have ADHD has allowed me to engage with my life in a way I wasn't able to before. It gave me a version of motherhood I'd never experienced. I became playful and energetic. Instead of being in a constant struggle of *managing*, I was finally able to relax and enjoy my life with my kids and my husband. When joy rather than shame or fear became my centering posture, the rest of my life got—dare I say?—easier.

I stopped waking up hating myself. I stopped chastising myself every moment of the day. Shame and guilt no longer owned my operating system. I forgave myself and became more forgiving of other people. I had become so judgmental and critical of others because of the way I viewed myself. When I saw myself through the lens of grace and understanding, I was able to see other people that way too. My anxiety and depression became background noise until one day I realized I couldn't remember the last time I hadn't been able to get out of bed. My confidence grew. I accepted myself and started to say the same thing God said when he breathed life into me for the first time: *It's good.*

This radical transformation was a wake-up call for me to care for my body—not *instead of* tending to my spiritual life, but as an extension of it. I realized how interconnected we are as physical and spiritual creations. To fully honor the image of God in me, I needed to honor the body he placed my spirit in. I stopped looking for a quick spiritual fix or a final physical solution and instead just looked for the next step. I chose to learn about my body and its specific needs. I took advice from nutritionists and doctors and tried well-tested methods. I moved the goalpost. I knew that my mental health would fluctuate, as would my physical health, but I decided that I would be kind to my body and my mind, no matter what.

In the winter, I eat foods I want, even if that means gaining weight. I move my body less when that's what my body needs, and I move it more, even if I don't feel like it, if that's what's right for my body that day. I buy clothes that fit my body and don't try to fit into a certain size. I sleep more. I run. I take supplements and drink lots of water. I go to bed at a reasonable hour and don't try to wake up before everyone else to "get things done." I stopped having a transactional relationship with food (as in "I ate a cookie, so I need to walk a mile!"). I build spiritual practices into my life to keep joy at the center. I lean into relationships that are safe and loving, and I make boundaries around the ones that aren't. I choose, every day, to learn how to better function in a world that isn't catered to me and my needs so I can live a life of abundant joy. When I stopped the treadmill of constantly trying to refine my body, I concluded that my body is not my enemy.

God didn't create us to be in animosity with the vessel he put us in.

God didn't create me to be in animosity with the vessel he put me in. In fact, I stopped thinking of myself as a vessel at all. My body isn't just a carrier of my soul from birth to death and on to eternity. It's a gift to be cared for and honored. Hating your humanity doesn't get you any closer to holiness. It just makes you hateful.

That's precisely why the theology of "I am, at my core, a rotten person" isn't compatible with the theology of "Love your neighbor" and "Judge not." We can't love when hate exists in our heart, even (and especially) when that hatred is directed at ourselves. We can't love our neighbors if we hate ourselves.

Your body isn't just a carrier of your soul from birth to death and on to eternity. It's a gift to be cared for and honored.

What does it look like to hate ourselves? When we compare ourselves to other people and always believe we are somehow worse. When we hate our bodies and are critical of them or constantly try to change them. When we engage in hypercriticism of ourselves and base our validation on what other people think. When we believe negative comments about ourselves without questioning their source or validity. When we downplay our strengths, gifts, and skills.

For Christians, self-hatred may begin as a quest to become more like Christ but leads to a truly mind-blowing amount of self-centered thinking. If you find yourself constantly thinking about yourself, how you're perceived, and what other people think about you, you have been bitten and devoured by the self-hate bug, my friend, and we're going to get you out of this.

Don't hate what God loves! And he loves *you*. As in, you right now, today, in this moment. All that you are and all that you've ever been and all that you'll ever be. Not because of anything you've done or because of how you've responded to him. Not because of who he *wants* you to be. He just loves you. Period. Full stop. No caveats.

When we accept that love, we begin to see ourselves differently—and treat ourselves differently. The love that exudes from the heart of the Father becomes our primary filter for our lives. Instead of seeing ourselves primarily as broken, we see ourselves as beloved, and our bodies become something we view with gratitude, regardless of how it functions, because when we believe that we are beloved, we accept our bodies and our minds as part of that belovedness. I believe that the better we feel and the healthier our self-image, the more we can reflect the love of God to the world around us.

Living this way requires awareness and attention. Most of us don't have bodies or minds that can function in neutral, so we have to keep pushing and pulling at the gears of our physical and spiritual lives. Sometimes that means finding a sustainable workout routine and sleep schedule. Sometimes it means learning our social capacity and practicing saying no and balancing our extracurriculars. Sometimes it means taking medication or committing to spiritual practices. It might sound like a lot of work, but it's possible to find a rhythm in all this. Over time, it feels less and less like survival and more and more like thriving.

Your body is not your enemy. Your mind is not your enemy. When you end the animosity between you and the body you live in, everything changes. Radical acceptance of who you are becomes radical *love* for who you are—a reflection of God's love for you.

Sometimes our theology gives us an out to not attend to our physical needs. I mean, how many of us have heard that we're getting brand-new, ideal bodies when we get to heaven? I'll never forget watching a man in our church (with a heart condition, for what it's worth) eat something his cardiologist would have called "career security" and saying through half-chewed food, "Can't wait to get my new body in heaven! Gonna be so thin! Ha!"

If you think your body doesn't matter because you're getting a new one, then you'll treat your body like trash. It's similar to ignoring our responsibility to care for the earth because, well, won't God just give us a new one someday? Such utopian theology, which promises a perfect earth and a perfect body in the future, creates a lack of care for the ones we live in now. Health advocates say, "You only get one body—treat it well!" Some Christians laugh and say, "Ha! That's what *you* think!" So we eat and drink, for tomorrow we die.

We downplay the significance of our bodily existence, despite the fact that Scripture emphasizes the sacredness of being human. Caring for our bodies isn't an elevation of the temporal over the spiritual but an integration of it. Paul calls our bodies temples of the Holy Spirit and implores us to care for them as such.[2] This passage is one of many in Scripture that show how our physical existence and our spiritual existence are one and the same. We cannot, and *should not*, attempt to compartmentalize them. How we treat our physical bodies affects them spiritually, and vice versa.

Scripture is full of instructions about what we put into our bodies, how we engage in sexual activity, and how we indulge in food or substances. While some of those are about our spiritual righteousness, they're not *only* about righteousness. They're also about what's best for our physical health.

A proverb implores us not to eat too much honey lest we vomit. Repeatedly in the Gospels, Jesus rests and acknowledges the need for others to rest as well. Scripture frequently points out the limitations of our bodies and the need for us to care for them well.[3] And who would know better what our bodies need than the one who created and breathed life into those bodies? But he didn't just create and breathe life, he also *took on our flesh*. A human body was good for the Creator. It is good for us as well.

Sometimes the church creates a radical theology in response to a radical movement within the larger culture. The emphasis on self-love and self-acceptance has, in some ways, become an out when it comes to accountability and growth. The pendulum swings widely both ways. The culture, tired of hypercriticism and self-hatred, has said, "We're not doing that anymore. We're gonna love ourselves!" Taken to an extreme, that mindset brings a person to reject any and all constructive criticism that can lead to growth and maturity. An overemphasis on self-love becomes self-elevation. On the flip side, an overemphasis on self-criticism becomes hatred. Both extremes lead to an unhealthy relationship with ourselves and the world around us.

What I'm suggesting is something that exists off the pendulum entirely. Not a response to the cultural temperature or a reaction to harmful theology, but a shaking of hands with the reality that we must exist without hatred for ourselves while also maintaining an openness to growth, even if it comes at the expense of our comfort. We can change without being motivated by shame or fear. We can love ourselves without allowing self-love and acceptance to prevent us from taking accountability for our actions. Humility is required to meet in the middle. A healthy life cannot and will not exist in extremes.

A life of peace and contentment requires both love and accountability.

Our bodies are meant to be cared for. We won't care for what we hate. Our minds are meant to be stewarded. We won't steward something if we don't think it has value. The way to care for our minds and bodies is a radical acceptance of God's posture toward us, toward our bodies, and toward our spiritual existence. And his posture toward us is one of love, care, and concern for our physical health, along with acceptance of where we are and who we are.

Radical love looks like these words in Romans: "I am persuaded that neither death nor life, nor angels nor rulers, nor things present nor things to come, nor powers, nor height nor depth, nor any other created thing will be able to separate us from the love of God that is in Christ Jesus."[4]

Radical care looks like these words in the letter to the Corinthians: "Don't you know that your body is a temple of the Holy Spirit who is in you, whom you have from God? You are not your own, for you were bought at a price. So glorify God with your body."[5]

Radical acceptance is found in integrating into our lives the truth that "while we were still sinners, Christ died for us."[6] These truths don't live on either end of a pendulum; they live in the steady, quiet center of God's heart. That's where we're invited to dwell.

I couldn't pray, will, or bootstrap away my anxiety, depression, PTSD, or ADHD. I couldn't change my body enough to make me love it. No matter how many self-hating mantras I scribbled into my journal and no matter how much I begged at the altar, I still woke up every day with the same mind. No matter how much I starved or exercised my body, it didn't become any more beautiful to me. Decades of hating myself didn't help me or make me holier. And none of those things ever would, because the problem was never that my body wasn't good or that my mind or heart were broken.

When I stopped thinking of my physical existence as an obstacle to overcome, life became something I enjoyed, not something I simply endured. When Jesus said he came to give us life in abundance, I believe that's what he meant. We're not just holding on through gritted teeth; we're embracing the freedom he offers so we can live a life of joy, peace, and contentment—right now. We aren't guaranteed perfectly healthy bodies. Our minds won't always be perfectly chemically balanced. We won't live without struggle or suffering. But the promise of Christ was never that our lives would be free of hard things. It was that we could have abundant life even in the midst of them.

Don't hate what God loves! And he loves *you*. As in, you right now, today, in this moment.

Abundance is accessible to us when we lean into his love for us and allow that love to inform our lives. I'm not talking about financial wealth, miraculously healed bodies, or lives free from trial. Abundance doesn't only exist in what we can hold in our hands. In this sense, I think about abundance as in the *quality* of our lives. Can we have happy and full lives even in bodies whose form and function are limited? Can we find healing from the effects of the trauma we've experienced? Can we move through life without hiding our bodies? Can we live in community and show up fully as ourselves and be loved and accepted that way?

I believe we can. I've lived in flight. I've lived in fright. I've lived in freeze. I've spent years unable to do more than limp to the end of the day and somehow find the will to get up and do it again the next day. I've hated my body and starved it. I've cursed my mind and numbed it. I've been lost in depression and homebound by anxiety. I've screamed at my husband and growled at my children. My life has been controlled by anger, fear, and sadness for more years than it hasn't.

And I have been cradled by God's goodness, at every step.

I begged God to heal me with finality, but he didn't. I begged for a miracle and didn't get one. I did everything I was taught to do spiritually and still suffered. When I decided to stop waiting for a miracle, I started to fight. I fought for joy. I fought for peace. I carved and cultivated my life to make the dark days easier. I started to treat my body like somebody loved it, even if I didn't. I treated my mind like it was made on purpose. And as I showed dignity and respect to my physical body, my spiritual heart strengthened. As I got healthier, shame disappeared from my framework. As I healed, I felt the delight of God. He delighted in me and I delighted in him, and in him I lived and moved and had my being and it was good.

Our experiences with our bodies and our self-image are as individual as our bodies themselves. I've struggled with both the way my body looks and the way it functions. Your war with your body probably looks different from mine, with different paths that will lead to healing the way you feel about yourself. Like me, you might have heard that your body is a temple and understood that to mean it's something to be strictly controlled. If you've struggled with your mental health or your neurodivergence, you might have been taught that those things are signs of spiritual weakness. You may have absorbed messages that your worth to the Kingdom of God is tied to the way you look or to your performance as a human being or to your mental strength. Maybe you've always thought that if you could just be stronger, holier, gentler, more disciplined, more of what everyone else seems to want from you, you would be accepted and loved, and a better asset to the Kingdom.

The tragedy in this way of thinking is that it causes us to ignore our bodies' signals, to silence our own internal cries for help, to try to pray away what might actually require medical treatment or rest. Our bodies aren't something to be mastered, and our minds aren't something to be overcome.

You're not a project; you're a person. And you are deeply loved—in every layer of your complexities.

How would the way we care for our bodies change if we stopped thinking of them primarily in terms of broken or bad and believed that they're first and foremost beloved? How would it change the way we engage with our pain, our joy, the good things and the hard things in our lives, if we believed that we are truly, unconditionally loved and wanted?

Our humanity isn't something we're meant to overcome but something that allows us to lean more into the presence and love of our Creator. Freedom doesn't come from having better bodies or fixing our brains or removing our limitations, whatever they might be. Liberation is found in saying, "I will learn to love, no matter what. I will fight for joy, in spite of what's fighting to steal it. I will build, not destroy. I will live honestly and embrace the love Christ offers me."

The thief may come to steal and kill and destroy, but you, my friend, are loved by the one who comes to give you *life*. You can take back what is rightfully yours. Your enemy isn't your body or your mind; the enemy is the thief. Your peace belongs to you. Your joy belongs to you. Your life belongs to you.

9

This Little Shame of Mine

It's Not Your Fault

THE ORANGE COUCH, SPRINGFIELD, MASSACHUSETTS, 2025

I'M WATCHING *GOOD WILL HUNTING* and my tears are flowing freely. It's the moment in the movie when Robin Williams's character, a therapist, looks at Will, his young, troubled client (played by Matt Damon), and says, "It's not your fault."

Will says dismissively, "Yeah, I know that."

Back and forth they go. "It's not your fault."

"I know."

"It's not your fault."

"I know."

The exchange continues until the weight of the words "It's not your fault" finally breaks past the walls that have protected this young man. Will collapses into the kind of crying that comes as a release of years of stored trauma, and Dr. Maguire pulls him into a tight embrace.

I'm crying just as hard.

I've wanted someone to say those words to me my entire life. I have carried so much blame and so much shame; it would be freeing to hear someone say that those things I'm ashamed about weren't my fault. I know these are just characters in a movie, but tonight, Robin Williams is saying "It's not your fault" to me. He might be the first person who ever has.

As the movie scene plays out and resolves, I'm lost in thought, traveling through space and time. I picture little Kristen and look at her with the same look on my face that Robin had on his. I pull her in and say, "It's not your fault." And if I'm already time traveling, then I might as well go to teenage Kristen's bedroom and sit on the floor with her and read her poems about how much she hates herself. I'll tell her, "It's not your fault." Then I'll go to the room where newly postpartum Kristen is crying in bed. I'll sit on the floor next to her while she cries herself to sleep because her baby won't stop crying and she's not producing enough milk. I'll hold her hand and say, "It's not your fault." Then I'll meet her outside the church and hold her shaking frame steady and tell her, "It's not your fault." I'll meet her in the NICU and whisper over beeping and buzzing machines, "It's not your fault."

But I don't have a time machine. I can't go back, and I know that. There's an indescribable pain in knowing something now that you didn't know then. But you couldn't have known what you know now if you hadn't had to learn it. As I'm sitting here, no longer paying attention to the movie, the images change. I'm no longer imagining a scenario; I'm seeing a vision. All those scenes from my life replay, but instead of older me saying, "It's not your fault," I see Jesus. He's sitting next to me on my bedroom floor, holding my hand and holding me up. And he's whispering, "It's not your fault."

"I know."

"It's not your fault."

"I know."

"It's not your fault."

"It's not your fault."

"It's not your fault."

He was always there, always telling me, always wanting me to believe that it was true—I just couldn't hear him. I thought Jesus blamed me. I thought he was on the prowl, making sure my sins were found out. I thought he was wagging his finger, threatening me with hell, disappointed in my choices and my desires. If I did hear "It's not your fault," I wouldn't have believed it. I would have said it was the devil giving me an excuse to not be accountable for my sin. But the blame was the lie. Jesus' presence and grace and love were the truth. *Are* the truth. He has been there every time—not retrospectively, but actively.

I am simultaneously relieved and filled with regret. I wish someone had told me. I wish I'd known. He was there and it wasn't my fault.

I started reading the Harry Potter series right after the second book was released. I checked it out of my school library in eighth grade, and I devoured it in a day. I quickly got my hands on the next one and looked forward to each new release until the last one came out my junior year of college. I have the warmest memories of being curled up in a chair, dead to the world, unwilling to stop turning pages until my eyes forced themselves shut. Up until a few kids ago, I reread the series every year, culminating with a movie marathon. When my kids were really into the series, we had so much fun being into the same thing at the same time, to a nerdy degree. Drinking Butterbeer with them at Universal Studios was one of the highlights of my life.

And so now you know. I'm a Harry Potter girlie.

I started hiding that fact when I became a youth pastor. I remember the Christian book burnings of the '90s. I've existed in Christian spaces long enough to have received every sort of comment about my literary interests. By the time my oldest son started to read the series, I was well versed in the craft of "how to respond to people when they tell you you're practicing witchcraft for reading Harry Potter."

One day my son innocently asked me, "Mom, is J. K. Rowling trying to make every kid a witch? That's what so-and-so said."

I blinked. That was new. But very on-brand of some Christians to uncover a global witch-recruitment strategy in a children's book. I try to reserve my snark and eye rolls around my kids, so I just said, "Well, what do *you* think?"

He paused for a second and said, "I think if she was trying to do that, she would have put it in her author bio." Astute observation, kid. No notes. My compliments to the chef who cooked that critical thinking skill into his preteen brain. (Me. I'm the chef.)

There are other things I've felt the need to hide from other Christians. Christian spaces often force us to hide parts of ourselves—our interests, our tastes, our instincts. When Zach and I left full-time ministry, I felt more freedom to just be myself and live my life. But when I became more of a public person online, that sense of freedom quickly went away. The more I shared my life and writing, the more people felt entitled to comment on it. I would innocently share about a book I was reading or a podcast I was listening to, and my inbox would explode with "concern" and demands for me to explain myself. "Careful!" one DM read, "That's a progressive author!" I was thirty years old at the time, and after I read that message, I went into the other room and asked my husband what *progressive* meant. He wasn't sure either. When I shared that Zach and I had "switched places" and he was going to stay home with the kids while I worked, people asked me if I was egalitarian. I shot my theologian friend a text: "What the heck is an egalitarian?"* I'm pretty sure I thought it had something to do with horses . . .

I didn't even know that there were categories of Christians. I didn't know you had to label yourself for other people to identify your particular brand of Christianity. The same friend who explained to me what *egalitarian* meant told me later, "It's okay that you read those books and listen to those podcasts, but every now and then you gotta drop some conservative, orthodox resources so people don't think you're theologically unsound."

There were so many rules and parameters. Now, not only did I need to focus on the work God had called me to, but I also had to be concerned about how that work was being perceived.

I've been accused of a lot of things in my life, but being disingenuous has never been one of them. When that pressure to be publicly well perceived fell on my shoulders, it sent me into the shadows. Trying to navigate these labels stifled my willingness to

* If you also didn't know this word, *egalitarianism* emphasizes shared leadership and mutual submission, with roles based on gifts rather than gender. This is contrasted with *complementarianism*, which emphasizes distinct roles, in which the husband leads and the wife supports.

pursue the call on my life. I was afraid. I wanted to succeed as a writer. I wanted to share the hope of Christ. I wanted to help hurting people. I mistakenly believed the only way to do that was to hide the parts of my life that might lead other people to believe my walk with Christ was less pure than someone else's. I tried to avoid conflict by shackling myself to rules that someone else made up and that self-appointed Christian watchdogs enforced.

Social pressure has a way of keeping us inside systems that require us to fracture ourselves to be included, accepted, respected, and valued. I lived in constant fear—fear that was placed on me by the expectations of a group of people who served the God who came to deliver us from shame but seemed to have forgotten that. They took the shackles Jesus had broken off and refastened them with a strict set of rules. They enforced the doctrine of "You can be free, but not like *that*. You can have fun, but not *that* way. You can enjoy things, but not *those* things." I had been living for Jesus all my life, but this was the most scrutinized I'd ever felt. At least when I was a kid, the rules were pretty clearly laid out. Now all the rules were unspoken—and punished harshly. I didn't know what words were safe, what tone was acceptable, what theology passed every single person's test. Every post was a potential trip wire. It was fear that provoked the warnings and the rules, and it was fear that made me hide. The yoke other people were putting on me was heavy. Hiding felt safer.

Social media has played a big role in creating a culture of faith that's less about our transformation in Christ and more about proving we've found the best way to be a Christian. The ease of access we have to one another and the way the algorithms show us content that elicits emotional reactions (like anger, shame, or fear) have created a culture that puts more and more demands on the way we live out our faith. We can't just follow Jesus anymore. We have to prove that we're following him the *right* way. We have to be the *right* kind of Christian. State our brand. Align our politics. Define our loyalties. Sign the charter.

We become disciples of whoever or whatever is in our algorithms, and unless we're doing regular spiritual audits, we might not be aware of how our faith is being transformed by the voices in our feed. It's so important for all of us, even those who use social media as a platform for ministry (me!), to use discernment and create boundaries around content that isn't producing good spiritual fruit in our lives.

We were designed for connection. There is long-suffering joy that comes from being known and seen and loved and enjoyed. But we can't access the privilege of that joy if we're in hiding. We can't connect with people and form bonds unless we're honest. It's hard to be honest about who we are if we don't believe that we're loved. It's hard to step out of hiding if we don't believe that we'll be safe away from the shadows.

Adam and Eve hid too. You could say they set the precedent for a shame response. After they disobeyed God, they ran and hid from him in the bushes. But God didn't start screaming at them when he saw what they'd done. His first move wasn't to cast them out of the garden or tell them what a disappointment they were to him. The first thing he did was to go looking for them. He showed up to do the same thing he'd done every day: walk with them in the garden. But they weren't there. So he called for them: "Where are you?" As if to say, *Where did you go? I'm right here.* Why were Adam and Eve so afraid? God didn't say, "If you do this, I will kill you." There was no threat. He just said, "Don't do that." And when he found them, he didn't yell at them. He "gentle parented" them out of the garden. Their decisions had consequences, but disconnection from the love of God wasn't part of that.

God isn't deterred by our shame, and he certainly isn't the author of it. Our shame comes from a dark place—it's born in the absence of God's light. The process of getting free from shame is a spiritual practice. Shame doesn't just wound—it distorts. It changes how we see ourselves, how we move through the world, and most insidiously, how we think God sees us.

My kids constantly catch me off guard with their awareness of mental health and trauma. My daughter, who's in fourth grade, will say things like, "I don't know why my teacher is so mean. Maybe something happened to her that makes her act angry when, really, she's just sad." My sons, who are both in middle school, will talk about the challenges their friends are going through and tell us when someone is depressed or has anxiety.

I go back and forth about how I feel about this. On the one hand, wow, is it great that they have the language and a basic understanding of these things. On the other hand, I wonder if it will overwhelm them at some point. Will the awareness of other people's emotions and trauma become a weight? Will they feel responsible for other people's struggles? Will they become people pleasers? Will they know the difference between depression and sadness? Nervousness and anxiety? Will they be quick to label themselves, resigning themselves to a life of struggle, not believing that treatment is available and there can be a way forward? It's uncharted territory, isn't it? To have an entire generation who has been raised with this kind of awareness and attunement?

Even so, I have to believe this prospect is better than the alternative: not being able to recognize mental health struggles at all. When I was growing up, things like depression and anxiety weren't part of everyday conversation like they are now. On top of that, they were considered spiritual issues. People who were truly committed to Christ didn't get depressed or suicidal, unless those feelings were temporary and circumstantial, coinciding with an event like a death or a job loss. And that's what they were: feelings. They weren't a condition or something you *had*—they were feelings, and feelings are passing. They also couldn't be trusted, because "the heart is deceitful above all things."[1] If depression and anxiety *were* a state, that state was a "stronghold" and strongholds were something only those who weren't surrendered to Christ experienced.

"Do not fear" is not a command; it's a comfort.

The solution to a stronghold was surrender. Lay it down at the altar. Repent. Pray. Sacrifice. Fast. Read God's Word. Have more faith. I did all of that, but I believed that the *degree* to which I did it was what mattered most. In the darkness of my depression, I didn't have the mental strength to do much more than make sure my kids didn't die under my care every day. How was I supposed to have the discipline and awareness to deepen my relationship with Christ? I felt so hopeless.

Now, of course, I see what a privileged belief framework that is. It's easy to believe that depression can only harm you if you let it if your mind has never struggled in this way. It's easy to look down on those who struggle and believe the narrative that they must have invited darkness into their life if yours has never been derailed by a chemical imbalance. It's easy to believe there's a simple solution if you've never had to live without one.

Whether the struggle is chemical, spiritual, or circumstantial, the church often doesn't know what to do with sad and anxious Christians. They're treated as outliers because they don't fit in the church's cleaned-up idea of what it means to follow Jesus. People say things like "*Most* Christians don't struggle with depression. *Most* Christians don't have anxiety." And they point to having faith as the reason. Outliers don't get to write the doctrines. So the outliers are the ones who suffer from the toxic shame those doctrines dish out.

There's a story in the New Testament that many a pastor and Christian leader have retold in the context of mental health, or really any chronic illness. We're going to call this "Using the Bible to Harm Sick People, Part 1." The story is found in John 5. Jesus went to the pool of Bethesda, where many people with sicknesses or disabilities gathered, hoping to be healed. The belief was that when the water moved (which was likely because it was a natural spring), there was an angel stirring the water. The first person to make it into the water after the water moved would, they believed, be healed of whatever ailed them.

When Jesus visited the pool, he came across a man who had been sitting there for thirty-eight years. Because of his disabilities (and because he didn't have anyone to carry him), he could never reach the water first. So Jesus went to him and asked, "Do you want to get well?"

The man explained his situation and why he'd been there for so long.

Jesus simply said, "Pick up your mat and walk."

And he did.

Christians have used Jesus' question to point to the reason we aren't healed. "Do you even *want* to be well?" someone might ask.

Or as one YouTube pastor put it, "Do you want to be well, or have you given up on the idea that God can heal you? Whether your problem is illness, a lack of willpower, or just lack of ability, we too often believe that our problem is chronic."

So if I just *want* it bad enough, God will heal me? If I'm not healed, it's because I don't believe I can be? I can't tell you how many times I've asked myself if I wanted to be well and not believed myself, because if I *actually* wanted to be well, I would be. The man at the pool didn't even know who Jesus was, and Jesus healed him. I *knew* Jesus and knew that he was capable of healing me and willing to do it, so if he wasn't, then it must be because I didn't actually want to be well.

We back ourselves into a spiritual corner, and instead of looking for resources that could help us, we look inside and try to will ourselves to be whole. We say we're trusting God and having faith, but in reality, we're placing our hope in our own ability to have enough faith to move God's hands. The trust isn't in his divinity and goodness but in our heart being worthy enough for his touch.

Whew. Are you exhausted by all this yet? Me too. But I'm not done.

In "Using the Bible to Harm Sick People, Part 2," we're going to look at a biblical phrase that's often swung at people who live with fear. The phrase "Do not fear" is used so frequently in the Bible that some Christians have made up outrageous assumptions about it. "It's in the Bible 365 times so that every day of the year we can be reminded to trust the Lord!" Except for leap year, I guess. Or the lunar year. Anyway, while it's true that these words are used a lot in Scripture, people tend to miss the reason God prompted almost every writer of the Bible to jot them down.

"Do not fear" is not a command; it's a comfort. The call to not be afraid isn't a chastisement for having a real, human reaction. When Jesus called Peter onto the water, he wasn't saying, "You big dummy! Don't be afraid, ya big sinner." When the Israelites were going to face armies triple their size, God's reason for saying "Don't be afraid" wasn't because they had no logical reason to fear. When Jairus's daughter died, Jesus didn't laugh at him for being distraught and afraid. For the record, it is against the nature of God to speak mockingly or dismissively toward anyone. And yet so many Christians take his words as doing just that.

Belief is an invitation. To accept it, we have to let go of the need to prove ourselves and step into the grace of God.

Sometimes people take the comfort and promise of God's presence—meant to soothe and assure us—and twist it into a tool of shame against those who are responding to their circumstances in a completely natural way. Fear does not unequivocally represent a lack of faith. Even if it did, that wouldn't change the nature of the words "Do not fear." Regardless of why we're afraid, the words were never intended to accuse us. They're meant to comfort us. In the same way we rock a child who wakes up with a nightmare and sing them a song or whisper, "It's okay. I'm right here. Don't be afraid," God holds us near and reminds us that we are safe with him. "I'm right here," he says. "Don't be afraid."

Sometimes I think we're more afraid of fear than we are of what scares us. I mean, if fear is equated with a lack of faith, of course we panic the second we have a question, a concern, a scary diagnosis, a betrayal, a heartbreak. We double down on "Do not fear," and we break ourselves apart. But if we're going to heal, we have to unlearn these assumptions that faith is something we need to prove and that grace is something we earn. Belief is an invitation. To accept it, we have to step into the grace of God, which is never held back from us.

Freedom isn't just knowing that we're safe; it's knowing that even if we feel afraid, we are still loved, held, and cherished. Never rejected. Never cast out. Never forgotten. Shame tells a different story. And one of the reasons people heap so much shame on others (whether intentionally or unintentionally) is because of the shame they feel about themselves.

It's tempting to make an idol out of righteousness and place our hope and faith in our ability to be good. We want to be pleasing to God, so we strive and beat ourselves bloody when we fail—even when our "failures" aren't failures at all.

As a young adult, I sat at the altar for hours and hours every chance I got, begging God to give me the gift of speaking in tongues. I was raised in a Pentecostal denomination that teaches that the evidence of being filled with the Holy Spirit is the ability to speak in tongues. If you wanted to be an ordained minister, you were required to regularly speak in your "prayer language." To be seen as an anointed person, worthy of ministry and influence, you had to have the evidence of a heart surrendered to the work of the Holy Spirit. Without this evidence, you couldn't experience the Holy Spirit's full power and effectiveness for ministry.*

You get pretty desperate when you believe God has called you into ministry but you don't have the gift that approves you for the

* This doctrine is based on Acts 1:8: "You will receive power when the Holy Spirit has come on you, and you will be my witnesses in Jerusalem, in all Judea and Samaria, and to the ends of the earth."

work. I was so desperate, I began to fake it. I didn't know I was faking it at first. I just did what the speaker told me to do.

"Close your eyes and repeat after me," he said. "Untie my bow tie. Untie my bow tie. Just say those words over and over and over again until it sounds like nonsense. Empty your mind and let the Holy Spirit take over."

It sounds ridiculous, but in the moment, I would have done *anything* to prove I was worthy of being used by God. So I rambled and cried and shook and declared, "I can speak in tongues!"

I wanted to speak in tongues not because of what it meant for me spiritually but because I was ashamed that I hadn't been given the gift. The lack of this gift meant I had sin in my heart that was making God hold himself back from me. It was my fault. I wouldn't need to hide if I could speak in tongues, so I spoke. However contrived it may have been didn't matter. No one checks the validity of your spiritual language.

For me, the litmus test I couldn't pass was speaking in tongues, but we probably all had (or have) community standards that we just couldn't live up to or access. A lot of churches have a political litmus test. To be a "real" Christian, you have to vote for a certain person and align with a certain party. Other churches assume that all women desire marriage and children and that something is wrong with them if they don't (or can't). There are church cultures where a pastor's authority should be accepted without question. If you have a concern or a question that signifies that you have a problem with authority, even if your intentions come from a genuine place (or maybe a bit of neurodivergence). Whatever the specifics in your community, when you're handed a checklist instead of an invitation, you'll never feel like you belong unless you are able to tick all those boxes.

I was ashamed that God hadn't given me the gift of tongues, so I performed what I didn't possess. Shame is a lens. Once it's set, everything gets interpreted through it. The shame lens makes us see everything as our fault and sometimes makes us accept abuse and mistreatment as what we deserve. Other times, shame can turn outward, leading us to push away people whose goodness and kindness make us feel even more unworthy of love. Because shame doesn't only make us hate ourselves; it also makes us suspicious of joy. It makes us critical of others. It keeps us looking for reasons to disqualify ourselves—and everyone else—from love. It tells us that we can't rest, that we can't be happy, that if we aren't constantly proving our worth, we'll lose it.

Sometimes we convince ourselves that the negative thoughts we have about ourselves are the voice of God or the Holy Spirit's conviction. Self-hatred feels righteous. We want to hate the things that God hates, and he is holy and righteous, so he must hate the things in us that aren't perfect. If we hate those things too, we think we'll be closer to righteousness. But those are lies. We live in shame and call it conviction. But in Christ, there is no shame and no condemnation.

I have lived in shame—shame over my lack of spiritual gifts, shame about my mental health, shame about my PTSD responses, shame about the way my brain works, shame about my lack of success, shame about my career failures, shame over my incapacities as a mother and a wife, shame about the way I am as a friend, shame about being an introvert, shame about saying the wrong thing at the wrong time, shame about the things I enjoy, shame about the way my body looks, shame about my clumsiness, my fears, my desires. I have never lived in shame about my sin.

In the moment, yes, of course, I'm ashamed of my choices. But I operate with the knowledge that my failures as a human are forgiven. They were forgiven before I made the choice, they're forgiven when I repent, and they're forgiven for eternity. Washed out. Clean. We're reminded repeatedly in Scripture not to hold on to the shame of our past but to rejoice that he has made us clean.[2]

Some of us feel more shame about the things we *didn't* choose than the things that we did. We may grow to resent the parts of us that were shaped by our environment, our biology, or our sheer survival instinct. The unchangeable attributes of who we are as individuals—like our personalities, our trauma responses, our family history, our bodies, our neurodivergence—are often the things we hate most about ourselves. But when we remove the lens of shame, when we finally let grace do the talking instead of guilt, the world softens.

We begin to heal when we no longer need anyone to tell us we're doing the right thing the right way. Instead, we can simply lock eyes with Jesus.

Shame keeps us hidden and afraid and angry and disconnected. But the love of God frees us. Embracing his love for us frees us to heal without fear and without seeking the validation of others. I began to heal, truly heal, when I no longer needed anyone to tell me I was doing the right thing the right way. I locked eyes with Jesus. I did as I saw him do. I let the Shepherd lead me.

When we dismantle shame, we're able to enjoy our lives without fear. We're free to take delight in things without feeling like someone's foot is on our neck. When we embrace our identity as beloved children of God, we welcome light and joy into our day. When shame doesn't control our movements, we can move more freely. We aren't looking over our shoulder anymore. We aren't self-flagellating every time we have the audacity to be human. We celebrate our life and live it with arms spread wide and a heart that has a normal resting beat.

"Do not fear" becomes a comfort and a promise.

"Do you want to get well?" turns into a hope that healing is possible.

"Be strong and courageous" becomes empowering.

"Don't worry" strengthens you.

When someone finally says, "It's not your fault," it's like the world tilts and our bodies don't know what to do with the sudden shift in gravity. That's why Matt Damon's character in *Good Will Hunting* doesn't believe it at first. That's why I didn't either. And yet when we finally let that truth sink in—when we let those words settle into the deepest cracks of who we are—we realize that maybe we were never meant to carry this weight in the first place. Perhaps there was a plan for shame all along and maybe, just maybe, that plan did not include our ruthless entanglement with it.

What does it feel like to be free from shame? It feels like waking up without dread. It feels like moving through the world without apologizing for taking up space. It feels like deep laughter—the kind that shakes your rib cage, makes you pee your pants a little, and reminds you that you're alive and that it's *good* that you are. It feels like letting yourself be loved without wondering if you've done enough to earn it.

When we shed shame, we don't become complacent, we become free. Free to walk in the light, free to live as we're created to live, free to let God transform us, not out of fear, but out of love.

10

True Wholeness Waits

You Are Loved and Safe and Free

LAVALLEY HOUSE, SPRINGFIELD, MASSACHUSETTS, 2024

I OPEN MY INSTAGRAM MESSAGES and start responding to a few over my morning coffee. My first book has been out for a few months, and the process has been emotionally exhausting. Retelling my traumas repeatedly has worn on me in ways I didn't expect. I feel as if I'm not made for the dialogues, the commentary on my life, the consumption of my spiritual formation as if I'm not even human.

Over the past couple of weeks, the messages have had a theme. People want to know why other authors I'm friends with have been quiet about my book.

At first, I think their questions are silly. My text messages are filled with support, gratitude, and celebration. But after a dozen or so messages, I start to think, *Maybe this is a problem. Maybe they hate me. Maybe I read the social cues wrong. Maybe I'm not who I thought I was to them. Maybe we're not even friends.* It goes beyond doubting myself—I'm confused, unsure if I should feel hurt or embarrassed.

I make a big, vulnerable mistake. I open Instagram and post a few stories. I announce that I'm taking a social media break and cite the book launch process and the sudden influx of questions about who is supporting or not supporting my book. I say, "I can't answer those questions for you and it's hurtful to me to come into my messages asking why someone isn't publicly posting about my book. I don't know. Ask them. I don't know."

I log off Instagram, delete the app, and breathe a sigh of relief.

The next day a text comes in.

Then another one.

Then an email.

I log onto Instagram in my browser and check my messages. More of the same.

Someone with a big platform is talking about what I said and insinuating that my priorities reveal my dissatisfaction in Christ. My heart sinks. I've been misunderstood. I'm humiliated. Someone sends me a post from another Christian content creator that's less obviously about me but close enough that she wonders if I think it is. Then I get a screenshot from a thread on Reddit from a few months prior, speculating on my friendships. It's all hitting at once.

And it sets the tone for the rest of my year. This is the year I find out how I'm perceived, and I continue to receive more commentary and criticism about my life, my work, my character, and the integrity of my faith.

There are the text messages meant for someone else but accidentally sent to me. There are the voice memos that I was never meant to hear. There are the reports from well-meaning friends and family members letting me know what my loved ones have said about me, why they haven't showed up for me, and what I should do to make things right.

Make things right? What did I do?

It feels a lot like evidences on a notepad.

I hear criticism about my work. About my writing. They think I don't talk about sin enough, or they don't like what I've said about the systems of church. They accuse me of not sharing enough context. Of not clearing enough names. I don't say enough. I say too much. I'm dramatic. I'm irreverent. I'm negative. I'm destructive. I'm too progressive. I'm not clear enough about where I stand. I'm too soft on things I should be hard about and too hard on things I should be soft about. I'm an offense. I'm a liability.

I'm gonna throw up.

If you could hear all those things said about you, to you, and in whispers around you, and not be affected by them, you'd have to be some kind of narcissist, I think. Or maybe someone who has their ego securely intact. That's not my story, but also—we're not supposed to know *that much* of what other people think of us. If you're a person who brushes up against the edges of what a "good Christian" is supposed to be and do and look like, you know the kind of pain I'm talking about.

I feel like my whole life has been a list of evidences against me. When I get this negative feedback, it's not about sin or character flaws. It's just . . . my vibes are off. It isn't about the details of what I say or teach; it's something about me.

But it isn't something about me.

It's *me.*

Like every human who has ever breathed, I want to belong. I want to be welcomed and accepted and celebrated, just like everyone else. But as it turns out, the worst thing you can be as a woman in Christian spaces is disruptive. It doesn't matter if the things you say are true if they aren't palatable. It took me a lifetime to realize that I was trying to find acceptance in all the wrong rooms. How many times did I walk into a room hoping to belong, only to walk out humiliated? How many conversations did I contort myself for, making sure I didn't say the wrong thing, ask the wrong question, or let too much of myself be seen?

The Kingdom of God isn't about making sure we fit somewhere—it's about belonging.

Those rooms never had space for me in the first place. They wanted me there, but only if I could fit their expectations. But I wasn't made to shrink. And I think I always knew that. I just didn't know I had permission to leave.

Jesus didn't tell the Samaritan woman to change before he sat with her. He didn't tell Zacchaeus to make himself more palatable before he entered his home. The Kingdom of God isn't about making sure we fit somewhere—it's about belonging. When Christ established his church, he didn't intend us to fight for belonging. That should be a given. This desire to belong isn't carnal. It isn't a sign of spiritual failure to want the people in your life to love you and support you. It isn't a sign of dissatisfaction in Christ to desire human things like success, acceptance, and love. *That's how we're wired.*

It goes against our divinely designed humanity to convince

ourselves that we're okay when we're not. It feels holier to say, "I'm satisfied in Christ" and pretend that nothing bothers us than to say, "I'm really sad about this." We can be satisfied in Christ and disappointed in other things at the same time. We can be deeply fulfilled by our work and our family and our career and still long for friendship and a place to feel welcome and wanted, inside and outside our home.

When my mom breathlessly told me, "We don't know who our friends are," it was a protective, sobering reality. Her words were true and, in their honesty, created a sacred moment in our kitchen in the middle of a relational storm. The malformation of my understanding about relationships didn't happen because of what my mom said, it happened because of the events that caused her to say it. It wasn't until I began to engage with the letters of Paul that I understood connection is a requirement for life in Christ. When unity is sabotaged and there is betrayal in a community, it is a sin against the nature of our creation and the nature of Christ's body—his bride, the church. I didn't want to need people in my life. I didn't want to have people close to me, even if I *did* need them. It feels easier that way. But it isn't good.

I had to stop trying to mold myself to fit what I thought other Christians wanted from me. It hurt too much to try to make myself those things and still sit at empty tables. Or to be given a seat, only to realize I didn't want to sit at the table while other people were waiting to be invited. I had to learn that my needs are not a problem and that if I'm not desiring sin, my desires aren't sinful. No Christian watchdog policing my behavior and interests and personality can undo what Christ has established in me.

Holiness doesn't isolate us; it integrates us. The places where I was finally seen and loved—where I was not just tolerated but celebrated and enjoyed—were the places where I healed. I became whole in the presence of Christ, carried in the hearts of his people who were kind, compassionate, and welcoming to me. Wholeness in Christ led to deep satisfaction in him.

That satisfaction can only come when we're confident in his love for us. That love (and the satisfaction in it) is what gives us the strength to stand up to injustice and abuse. It's the reason we can step aside and celebrate other people's wins. It's what emboldens us to stand firm in what we believe and what he has called us to do, even when we're misunderstood or mistreated because of it. It's what gives us the grace to forgive without apology and to see ourselves the way he sees us, not the way other people perceive us.

Holiness doesn't isolate us; it integrates us.

The more I learned to view myself as loved by God and the more I leaned into the steadiness of his presence, the more I was able to view the world through the lens of his love. When I stopped believing that he dangled his presence and love and acceptance like a carrot, the less worried I became about what I did and the more I focused on who I was and who I was becoming. And because I believed that I was worthy of being loved and accepted by the perfect Creator, I started to act like I was worthy of being loved and accepted by his people as well. If they couldn't acknowledge my worth as an image bearer and see my devotion to the work he called me to do and maybe, I don't know, give me the benefit of the doubt, then those weren't relationships I needed to pine for.

God's formation of our heart changes the way we behave. This is a process that lasts our entire lifetime. The more God forms me, the less shame and hatred I feel for myself. The more he forms me, the less I feel like I have to beat myself up to do good. I don't have to be convinced to do good or be good; his goodness flows out of me as a result of his presence in my life. My goodness is both a response to his love and an impartation of his image in me. I'm good because he's good and he made me, and he has made me good and he *makes* me good.

We can't make ourselves holy. We're made that way as we pursue Christ. We are the righteousness of God. Let's return to this for a minute. I don't think we've sat with it long enough. In the Bible, we are never called "the sin of the devil" or "the wickedness of the earth." We're called "the righteousness of God."[1] This is *profound.*

In 2 Corinthians 5, Paul names the ache we carry for new bodies, for wholeness, for a world made right. And then he says this: "If we are out of our mind, it is for God; if we are in our right mind, it is for you." In other words, you can be a certified Jesus freak, but when it comes to other people, you better come correct. Spiritual fervor isn't an excuse for emotional and relational harm. Listen, you can take the girl out of the Pentecostal church, but you can pry my hanky out of my cold, dead hands, 'cause I'm waving it around right now. As the people say, "PREACH!"

But we aren't even at the best part yet. Paul said, "He made the one who did not know sin to be sin for us, so that in him we might become the righteousness of God." Did you catch that? We become the righteousness of God. Not that we *have* his righteousness. Or that we are trying to *be* righteous. But that we *are* his righteousness. As in, if God was introducing us to his friend, his friend would say, "Oh, God, I'd like you to meet my son." And God would be like, "Wonderful to meet you. I'd like you to meet my Righteousness." And then he'd point to you.

When we decide to follow Jesus, the righteousness of God is

credited to us. We don't have to earn it. We don't have to strive for it. It's ours. It's who we become when we become his.

Here's what this means for your life:

1. Your entire identity shifts. You are no longer defined by your sin or mistakes. You're defined by your adoption into the family of God. You are holy and blameless before him.
2. Your goodness—your *righteousness*—is imputed to you when you are reborn into Christ's Kingdom. This isn't because of anything you did or anything you *should* do. It's a gift.
3. Your relationship with God is no longer broken by shame. You don't have to hide in the bushes anymore. He's showing up for the walk with you, same as he does every day, and when you come out of hiding, he's going to take care of you. You no longer need to condemn yourself, beat yourself up, or be afraid of God's wrath and judgment. You're safe with him, and you're welcomed into his presence with open, loving arms.
4. You have an embodied faith that empowers you to live out God's will for your life. As you pursue God's goodness and wholeness, he transforms you, aligning your desires with his. You can hold your head high, confident in the love he has for you, knowing there's nothing you can do that will separate you from that love. You can face hardship and criticism without allowing it to shape your identity. You can rejoice in his provision and abundance (whatever that looks like in a given season) without waiting for God to take it all away.

5. You can lean into joy, peace, and contentment. That doesn't mean your life will be without hardship, doubt, or struggle, but you'll be able to hold the tensions and nuances of faith and human existence with grace and hope. You no longer need God to be one thing or the other. You can trust his character and trust that no matter what happens to you or what mistakes you make along the way, no circumstantial evidence will change the truth of who God is and how he cares for you.

At least we *hope* all these things will be true for every person who decides to follow Jesus. This is maybe a bit of an idealistic list. If it were unequivocally true for everyone, we wouldn't really need to write books about overcoming shame and broken identity, now, would we? Not everyone who labels themselves a Christian allows themselves to be transformed. Sometimes that "inherit righteousness" becomes a "get out of jail free" card for people who are determined to do what they want to do, no matter what.

I learned all about inherited righteousness when I was three years old. My grandfather and I always had a special bond. All the cousins will argue it, but from an early age, I knew I was his favorite. One day I was jumping off his recliner over and over again, even though my mom kept warning me to stop. Of course, I didn't listen, and I knocked over Papa's lamp, shattering the glass shade.

My mom was furious. "You're going to tell Papa what you did," she said, making sure I knew just how disappointed he would be.

When Papa got home, she marched me into the living room and said, "Daddy, Kristen has something to tell you."

He sat in his chair, pulled me onto his lap, and waited. "Tell him what you did, Kristen."

I puckered my lip and lowered my head. "Papa . . . I broke your lamp."

Papa immediately wrapped his arms around me and said, "That's okay, baby!"

Knowing she'd been outplayed, my mom protested, "Daddy! She's supposed to be learning repentance!"

The story goes that I looked up at my mother from where my head was resting safely on Papa's shoulder and gave her the smuggest look a person can give, like *So we all know where we stand now, right?*

I had inherited righteousness with Papa, and I knew it. And for the record, I never forgot it.

That kind of safety, the kind where you're fully known and loved, can form us in a few different ways. It can make us careless, assuming there won't be consequences for our actions, or it can become the foundation that transforms us. Realistically, I didn't learn any big lessons from breaking Papa's lamp, but his consistent love and tenderness with me over the course of my life made me want to never disappoint him.

Spiritually speaking, there's a tension between the knowledge that we are called to act in accordance with what we know is righteous and the inherent righteousness that is given to us because of Christ. Because of the new title we've been given, we'll act in a way that reflects the righteousness of God, who has given us his image. The goodness that has been bestowed on us by spiritual birth is also the motivator to live a life consecrated to Christ and dedicated to reflecting him in our life.

Where we get this twisted is the belief that God's love hinges on our ability to achieve righteousness, which of course, we cannot achieve on our own. Adam and Eve tried to hide their own nakedness, but their hastily sewn fig leaves weren't enough. They needed God's intervention and provision to cover them in a more sufficient way. God knew we'd never be able to be holy on our own because he didn't create us to be holy on our own. He gave us *his* holiness instead. He created a path toward righteousness—a path that doesn't depend on our own efforts and achievements.

We weren't created to be slaves to our sin or subjects of God's wrath; we were created for his pleasure. When we believe that he is good and kind and faithful, we respond by pursuing the wholeness only he can provide. This is what the relentless pursuit of wholeness looks like. Not a striving, not a proving, but a return to what has always been true: We are loved. We are safe. We are free.

I thought righteousness was something I had to prove. I thought if I could be good enough and holy enough, if I made all the right decisions, my holiness would earn me respect, honor, and value in the Kingdom of God and the communities I was in. If I was good, I'd be safe. But I got tired. The striving for worth burned me out and nearly cost me my belief in God entirely. When I stopped trying to prove my worth and started living *from* it, everything changed.

When we stop trying to prove our worth and start living *from* it, everything changes.

I stopped asking permission to take up space. I stopped trying to make myself smaller and more digestible for other people. I stopped hiding the things I enjoy and stopped feeling the need to baptize them with purpose. I didn't become reckless, I just got free. I loved more wholly, I forgave more easily.

My rest was deeper, my spiritual posture taller. I stopped living in the narratives and perceptions of others and accepted an identifier from one, and only one: the God who calls me his beloved and his righteousness.

I think about the multiverse a lot. Is there some version of me who grew up in one church, where my dad was the pastor, where *he* was loved and *we* were loved? Did multiverse Kristen grow up with relational and financial security? Does that version of me have secure attachment? Does she struggle with her mental health? How different would my life have been if my childhood hadn't been so deeply affected by my early expulsion and rejection from so many corners of God's house?

As it stands, the multiverse isn't a thing, and even if it is, I exist in the timeline where all that happened and I have to live with the consequences. I was formed in Christian spaces and malformed by more than just the big events that derailed my life. It's often the seemingly innocuous subtleties that indefinitely shape our beliefs. When some parts of the community are good, we tend to just roll with it, not recognizing that some of the less obvious aspects are unhealthy and detrimental to our spiritual life.

We grow into our godliness; we aren't born with it. As we grow and mature, we become more like him, but we have to be willing to change, adapt, rethink, and reevaluate. We acknowledge our malformation, name it, and begin the process of reforming our faith into something more closely aligned with what is true and right. Malformation to reformation. Deconstruction to reconstruction. Sinner to sanctified. Tomayto, tomahto.

When Jesus interacted with the broken and the hurting, his first task was to restore their dignity. Just as God clothed Adam and Eve in the garden, Jesus removed the shame of sin and sickness and talked to people as individuals worthy of respect. The Samaritan woman, the woman who bled, tax collectors, those with leprosy—he gave them dignity, healed them, fed them, and let the testimony of his work speak. He didn't say, "Stop sinning and you'll be healed." He healed them, protected them, restored their dignity, and then, when applicable, said, "Go and sin no more." Our godliness is a response to his love, not a requirement for it.

The more I embodied that belief and lived my life as a response to God's love rather than a desperate plea for it, the less I obsessed over my sin. And as a by-product of that, the less I thought about *other* people's sin. God never intended our primary focus to be on our own brokenness. He didn't call us to refine ourselves, hate ourselves, or change ourselves. He is the one who transforms our hearts and gives us the opportunity to step into his freedom and live from that freedom in a relentless pursuit of wholeness.

We were created for joy, and joy is something God longs to give us. Joy exists in the deeply connected relationships we have with each other, rooted in the connection we have with our Father. We can't have wholeness without connection. Our human design requires connection with other people, with the earth, with God, with ourselves. When sin entered the atmosphere of our human existence, it broke all those connections. The love of God is an invitation to repair that brokenness. He's going to make it all new one day, but he's also making it all new right now, with me and you. We don't have to toil

Our godliness is a response to his love, not a requirement for it.

from one day to the next, bemoaning our sinful nature, allowing shame to keep us in hiding, giving pain the pen to write the story of our lives.

Christ took on flesh and, in his flesh, conquered pain and death. Every time he said the words "You've heard that it was said," he showed us a new way. A *better* way. A more complete way to live in his truth, with his character, as a reflection of him, and in the image of his Father on this earth. He offers his love abundantly and his grace freely, and he requires that we do the same. Life with Christ is not a burden. It's not a weight. It should not be characterized by anger, resentment, regret, exclusion, isolation, or checklists. When our faith is embodied and integrated into every aspect of our being, our lives can be beautiful, in spite of our circumstances, our pain, our scars, our loneliness, and our bruised beliefs. He makes us new. He makes us whole. One day, yes, but also, right now, as we live and breathe and have our being in him.

Wholeness isn't an abstract spiritual idea. It doesn't only exist in the utopia of eternal life. It's also a present reality offered to us through the work of Christ. It's waking up without shame on our back. It's faith without a foot on our neck. It's being in a room full of people who don't like us and still feeling fully confident in our worth. It's worshiping freely, not because we're trying to prove our devotion, but as a response to God's love. It's walking away from a painful conversation without staying up all night replaying every word, regretting the said and the unsaid. It's resting in the truth, every day, that we're known and loved completely. It's laughter without justifying our joy. It's crying without sanctifying our tears. It's looking at the old versions of ourselves with tenderness, not regret. It's recognizing that even when we didn't realize it, we were becoming free. And we still are.

In spite of my pain and malformation in the church, I just can't quit her. Even when Christians criticize me for walking with people the church often forgets or casts out, I refuse to stop setting tables, pulling up chairs, and welcoming the weary, the disillusioned, the deconstructed, and the misunderstood. I have lived through more relational pain inside the church than I will probably ever write down, but I'm still here. I still believe in the bride of Christ.

The prophet Jeremiah faced physical abuse, public humiliation, and internal conflict for doing what God had called him to do and saying what God had called him to say. Still, despite the cost, the words burned inside him and he couldn't stay silent. I've found myself relating to Jeremiah's words: "I say, 'I won't mention him or speak any longer in his name.' But his message becomes a fire burning in my heart, shut up in my bones. I become tired of holding it in, and I cannot prevail" (Jeremiah 20:9). I've looked everywhere else, and I keep coming back to the single question, "Where else would I go?"

When you're hurt inside the walls of a church, at the hands of a brother or sister in Christ, or a whole community of them, you can feel like the answer is to find fulfillment and healing outside the church. And for some of us, that's necessary for a time. You can't heal in the same place you were hurt. Sometimes you need distance. I had to leave the building to find the bride. And the bride is who pulled me back into Jesus.

I metabolized theology that made me feel like I had no worth, but those who carry Christ in them have been the theology of grace, mercy, compassion, and hope for me. Although I have been wounded by some shepherds who were called to gently lead me, I love, respect, and honor the shepherds who lead like the shepherd

Jesus. And even though people have broken me in ways that have left deep, lasting scars, I pull people in closer than ever before, and I live without fear of pain.

This is how God has called us to live: in community with one another, being spiritually formed and repaired together so we can grow in righteousness and be the hands and feet of Christ. The response to his love is to *love*—each other and ourselves—and to repair a world that has been broken and malformed by sin and suffering. This is the path to wholeness. This is the way we get free. And you *will* be free.

There is a version of you that you haven't met yet.

She is free to live with and after pain.

She glows from the inside out.

She isn't afraid of people.

She is open to friendship and guarded in all the right ways.

She is a protector—but not just of herself anymore.

Her yeses and noes are more confident, free from shame. Full sentences.

She dances easily, cries freely, and doesn't apologize for taking up space.

She's someone people come to when they need to feel safe.

She doesn't just notice the threats in the room; she notices the beauty too.

She is scarred and her hair is gray, and she loves that because it means she lived . . . and survived.

Her spiritual community is much more ragtag than it used to be, because the ragtags held her when no one else would. She honors those around her without requiring them to pass any spiritual litmus tests or align with a certain set of homogeneous beliefs. She is happy, truly. She isn't waiting for one day. Although she has hopes for the future, she doesn't need anything to change or get better because *she* is changing, and as she morphs, so does her environment. She's not pulling weeds anymore, she's planting flowers. She *is* the garden. And everywhere she goes, life blooms.

You don't need a faith that's never been shaken to experience the wholeness that's available to you. Wholeness isn't the absence of pain or the presence of perfection. It's also not an impossible ideal or something reserved for someday in heaven. When you accept yourself—flaws and quirks and all—and understand your worth in light of God's unconditional love, your wounds can heal and your spiritual malformations start to lose their grip on you. In the process, wholeness becomes a much more tangible reality. Being whole is about spiritual, emotional, mental, and physical wellness, and it is sourced in our belief that God doesn't see us as failures but as his beloved children: loved, redeemed, and reconciled to him.

Wholeness is the integration of the parts of yourself that can't be changed and the parts that need refining. In that integration, you'll experience peace that surpasses understanding—peace that frees you from the need to strive. You won't be flawless, but you won't aim to be anymore. When sin is put in the right light, shame loses its grip on you. You begin to see yourself with the same compassion that God extends to you, and as you do, you're more able to offer compassion to others as well.

Sin might have fractured us, our relationships, and our intimacy with God, but sin doesn't get to write our stories. Wholeness isn't something we earn, but something we return to. It's God's desired state for us. Rather than seeing ourselves through the lens of our sin and brokenness and failures, we are invited to return to how he always intended us to be: with him in the garden, walking and talking together, with nothing between us.

I thought God required a lot more of me than he actually did. So I hated myself, hid myself, and lived a half-life, waiting for his blow, never fully living the way he called me to live. When I gave up that pursuit, I thought it meant I was giving up my faith. And for a long time, that's what it felt like. If I couldn't have Jesus without hating myself, I didn't want him. I couldn't. It was costing me my life, my marriage, my family.

But along the way, I found that life in Christ *is* wholeness. Anything else isn't him. You don't have to prove that you're worthy of love—you already are. You don't have to break yourself to be holy—God has already decided that you are. You don't have to earn belonging—you belong by nature of your spiritual birth. You don't have to hide yourself—you're fully known, fully seen, and fully loved.

Faith shouldn't feel like someone's foot is on our necks. God's love makes room for the whole of who we are. He doesn't demand perfection, just presence. He doesn't silence our struggle; he sits with us in it.

Growing up saved didn't protect me from shame, self-hatred, or spiritual confusion, but it did give me faith language. It gave me stories to wrestle with, mysteries to wonder about, and scaffolding to build my belief on.

To grow up saved, wherever we mark the pivot point in our journey with God, is to be shaped by our proximity to something the generations before us have tried to understand. It's the lifelong, tender work of becoming whole. Of returning to ourselves. Maybe we don't have to outgrow whatever faith frameworks we inherited. Maybe we just grow into a faith that can hold our pain, our healing, our questions, our wounds, and our wonder.

Faith doesn't highlight our brokenness; it leads us to our wholeness. It whispers to us, again and again, "You are loved—right here, right now, as you are."

That's the kind of saved I'm growing into.

It's yours to grow into too.

Author's Note

WHEN I STARTED TELLING PEOPLE I was writing a book that dug into my childhood and all the ways the faith of my childhood formed me and failed me, there was a bit of a collective "Ruh-roh." And fair enough. Writing honestly about what hurt you without sounding like you're blaming the people who raised you is no small task. And since I was raised in a pastoral family, you can imagine how a story like mine overlaps with a lot of lives.

To the best of my ability, I have tried to tell what was true for me—with grace and generosity.

I've never written about my childhood quite like this before, and I wasn't interested in writing a takedown. I never felt the need or desire to. I just wanted to tell the truth about how some of the messages I internalized as I was growing up saved made me miserable and anxious, and made faith feel cruel. So many of us who grew up this way have swung wildly on the faith pendulum, unsure of where it's safe to land. I wanted to show that faith doesn't have to feel like suffocation. You can love God and follow him without feeling like you're being crushed by him.

We're all made up of pieces of other people. We are patchwork quilts stitched together from the voices, habits, wounds, and wisdom of the ones who have shaped us. Our accents. Our humor. Our fears. Our faith. And so there is no one to blame for my pain and no single person to credit for my healing. It's everyone. It's no one. And sometimes, it's the same people for both.

The point is this: It happened. It hurt. And now my life is beautiful—because of it and in spite of it.

Acknowledgments

JUST LIKE A LIFE IS MADE of the people who touched it, so is a book. This is the part where I thank the people who made this one possible.

To my parents: I'm forever grateful for the ways you stretched your own faith frameworks, because it gave me the courage to do the same. So really, if anything I say (in this book or outside of it) ever makes you mad, it's actually kind of your fault. You made it okay for me to push and question and wrestle with what I believe about God. Thank you for introducing me to the faith that still informs my life. I'm well aware of what a gift it is to have never known a day without Jesus.

To my husband: Thank you for being the first person to make me feel safe enough to take off my masks. I didn't know how many I was wearing until I met you. There's no way you knew that building a life with me would mean spending your life surrounded by (and raising) a bunch of neurodivergent girlies, but I'm lucky to have you and so are our girls. You make the world a kinder and safer place for people like us.

To my kids: Thank you for being the kind of children who don't care that I'm an author and still ask me, regularly, if I'm ever gonna get a job.

To my siblings: We grew up saved *together*, so my story will never be the full story. I'm grateful for the ways you've walked your own paths with Jesus, because they've inspired and challenged my own. Performing fully choreographed human videos in the living room, having to learn harmony to sing "Lily of the Valley" anytime Mom felt led, and simultaneously being the worship team, the children's ministry, and the sound booth techs—that's a special kind of spiritual formation most people aren't privy to. Those were my favorite days. Growing up with you was a joy.

To my sister, Abby Palow: Even though I've been writing since before you were born, you were the first person I ever wrote *for*. I was only thirteen when I started addressing my journals to you. You were my first audience—the first person I wanted to protect, guide, offer something better to. I hoped you might learn from my mistakes, though I'm not sure how much a teenager can really teach or how often another teenager listens. Still, those letters were the beginning. And now, all these years later, I find myself wanting to be more and more like *you*. Your honesty and loyalty are rare gifts. Thank you for having my back and for sharing your courage with me. This book would not be what it's become without you.

To my publishing team: Thank you for your work in bringing this second book into the world. Each project teaches me something new and stretches me in ways I don't want to be stretched, but I'm grateful for it nonetheless. Thank you for your partnership, time, and commitment to getting these words into people's hands. A very special thanks to Kara Leonino, for understanding my voice and my heart and honoring both with so much care.

To my agent, Rachel Jacobson: Who would've thought a little

DM I ignored for months would lead us here? Thank you for your patience, for your belief in my voice, and for waiting until I was ready to tell my stories on my own terms. Your advocacy means the world to me.

To K.J. Ramsey: Your friendship and gentle presence in the writing of this book has been a lifeline for me. Nearly every word was written under the smoke of the Palo Santo you sent me, so I think you deserve at least partial credit (or blame?) for what made it onto the page.

To every kid who grew up saved but never felt like they got it right: This is for you. For the guilt you carried, the questions you stifled, and the brokenness you thought was your identifier. I hope you've found God to be kinder, gentler, and closer than you ever imagined he could be.

To the '90s Christian culture that gave me a faith I needed to heal from and is probably the main reason for my anxious attachment, this is for you. You gave me a God who was hard to please and a faith that made me hate myself, but I guess I can't really blame you. If I thought Jesus would return at any moment, leaving only a pile of neatly folded clothes behind, I'd probably have pressured a generation into setting themselves on fire for him too. Consider this book a truce.

To you, dear reader: Especially those who have followed my work, shared your own stories, and whispered "Me, too" in living rooms, at retreats, in writing workshops, and in the quiet corners of the internet, thank you. I don't take it lightly that you trust me with your wounds and your wonderings. This book is mine, but it's yours too. It's stitched together with your courage, your questions, and your audacity to hold on to hope. I'm so grateful to be walking this road with you.

And finally, to little Kristen: You tried so hard to get it right—*all the time*. But it was never really yours to get right. You were too little to carry all that weight, and I wish I could go back and tell you that. I know how heavy it was. I'm sorry you thought that was what you had to do. Thank you for holding on to Jesus long enough for me to find my way back to you. Thank you for being tender and brave and imaginative and stubborn. You started writing to make sense of the world, and you kept writing because you believed there was more. You were right. The words you scribbled into journals became the trail that led me back home to myself. I carry little pieces of you with me, always.

Notes

CHAPTER 1: FRIENDS ARE FRIENDS FOREVER (UNLESS YOU BACKSLIDE)

1. Berna Güroğlu, "The Power of Friendship: The Developmental Significance of Friendships from a Neuroscience Perspective," *Child Development Perspectives* 16, no. 2 (2022): 110–117, https://doi.org/10.1111/cdep.12450.
2. Sarah Schuster, "The 4 Trauma Responses: Fight, Flight, Freeze, and Fawn," *Health*, October 17, 2023, https://www.health.com/fight-flight-freeze-fawn-8348342.
3. Jim Wilder and Ray Woolridge, *Escaping Enemy Mode: How Our Brains Unite or Divide Us* (Northfield, 2022).
4. Jeffrey Kranz, "All the 'One Another' Commands in the NT [infographic]," Overview Bible, March 9, 2014, https://overviewbible.com/one-another-infographic/.
5. John 14:12, NIV.

CHAPTER 3: DARE YOU TO DOUBT

1. Anne Solomon, "Spiritual Abuse," accessed May 26, 2025, https://www.spiritual-life.co.uk/single-post/2016/02/12/spiritual-abuse.
2. David Johnson and Jeff VanVonderen, *The Subtle Power of Spiritual Abuse: Recognizing and Escaping Spiritual Manipulation and False Spiritual Authority Within the Church* (Bethany House, 1991).
3. In 50 percent of cases studied, spiritual abuse led to depression, and 33 percent of those affected reported suicidal ideation. Victims have also reported phobias, social disorders, aggression, and dissociative disorders. Breanna Barnes, "Religious Abuse: Impact on Mental Health and Development," California State University, Northridge, May 2020, https://scholarworks.calstate.edu/downloads/tb09jb36z.

4. Because so many patients present with symptoms of PTSD after experiencing spiritual abuse, a new syndrome was defined in 2011. Religious trauma syndrome (RTS) is a formal diagnosis given to people who have any combination of these symptoms resulting from their experience in high-control, abusive religious environments: confusion, difficulty making decisions or thinking critically, dissociation, confusion about their identity, anxiety, panic attacks, depression, suicidal ideation, guilt, grief, loneliness, purposelessness, trouble sleeping, eating disorders, nightmares, sexual dysfunction, substance abuse, rupture of family or friendships, inability to hold a job, financial stress, relational dysfunction, sexual immaturity, and in children, emotional, intellectual, and social delays. See Sumeet Singh et al., "Religious Trauma Syndrome: The Futile Fate of Faith," *Industrial Psychiatry Journal* 33, suppl. 1 (2024): S309–S310, https://doi.org/10.4103/ipj.ipj_87_24.
5. Ming Zhang et al., "The Dual Facilitatory and Inhibitory Effects of Social Pain on Physical Pain Perception," *iScience* 27, no. 2 (2024), https://doi.org/10.1016/j.isci.2024.108951.
6. Particularly the dorsal anterior cingulate cortex (dACC) and anterior insula (AI).
7. Brian D. McLaren, "The Four Stages of Faith," accessed May 26, 2025, https://brianmclaren.net/wp-content/uploads/2022/12/Four-Stages-1.pdf.
8. Philip Yancey, *Reaching for the Invisible God: What Can We Expect to Find?* (Zondervan, 2000).
9. 2 Peter 3:9.

CHAPTER 4: WWJD? HE'D LIKE YOU

1. Daniel J. Siegel, *The Developing Mind: How Relationships and the Brain Interact to Shape Who We Are*, 3rd ed. (Guilford Press, 2020).
2. *Inside Out 2*, directed by Kelsey Mann (Pixar Animation Studios, 2024).
3. Rae Jacobson, "How Girls with ADHD Are Different: And the Emotional Costs of Being Overlooked," Child Mind Institute, last reviewed or updated March 17, 2025, https://childmind.org/article/how-girls-with-adhd-are-different.
4. "Effects," What Is Child Trauma?, The National Child Traumatic Stress Network, accessed May 29, 2025, https://www.nctsn.org/what-is-child-trauma/trauma-types/complex-trauma/effects.
5. Curt Thompson, *The Soul of Shame: Retelling the Stories We Believe About Ourselves* (InterVarsity Press, 2015).
6. 2 Corinthians 5:17, 21; 1:21-22; 1 Peter 2:9; 1:15-16; Colossians 3:12; Isaiah 1:18; Ephesians 1:7; Romans 8:1.

7. Revelation 12:10; 1 John 2:1; Romans 9:25; 2 Corinthians 5:21.
8. Romans 12:2; 2 Corinthians 3:18.

CHAPTER 5: ACQUIRE THE FIRE, SURVIVE THE BURN

1. Patricia McDougall et al., "The Consequences of Childhood Peer Rejection," in Mark R. Leary, ed., *Interpersonal Rejection* (Oxford University Press, 2001), 213–247.
2. Jude Cassidy, "The Nature of the Child's Ties," in Jude Cassidy and Phillip R. Shaver, eds., *Handbook of Attachment: Theory, Research, and Clinical Applications* (Guilford Press, 1999).
3. Beverly James, *Handbook for Treatment of Attachment-Trauma Problems in Children* (Lexington Books, 1994).

CHAPTER 6: IT'S NOT A DEMON, IT'S DEPRESSION

1. 2 Samuel 9:1-13.
2. Mark 2:1-12.
3. 1 Kings 19:1-18.
4. Isaiah 42:3.
5. Matthew 11:28.

CHAPTER 7: NOT LEFT BEHIND

1. 1 Corinthians 15:33; Hebrews 2:1.
2. Matthew 7:2.
3. Psalm 23:6, ESV.
4. John 10:10; 15:11; Psalm 16:11; 37:4; Matthew 7:7; Zephaniah 3:17.
5. C. S. Lewis, *The Lion, the Witch and the Wardrobe* (HarperCollins, 1950), 80–81.
6. God as protector: Hosea 11:10; Psalm 18:2; 3:3; 125:2; John 10:9; Job 1:10; Isaiah 26:4; Proverbs 18:10. God as nurturer: Deuteronomy 32:11; Matthew 23:37; Isaiah 66:13; 49:15; Psalm 22:9; Hosea 13:8.
7. Licensed marriage and family therapist Saba Harouni Lurie defines this term as referring to "the type of parenting that results in children 'walking on eggshells' in response to their parent's unpredictable behavior and outbursts." Ashley Laderer, "What Is Eggshell Parenting?" Charlie Health, August 14, 2023, https://www.charliehealth.com/post/what-is-eggshell-parenting.

CHAPTER 8: I KISSED HATING MYSELF GOODBYE

1. 1 Kings 19.
2. 1 Corinthians 6:19-20.

3. Proverbs 25:27; Mark 6:31; Luke 10:38-42; Mark 5:43; John 21:12; Luke 8:55; Matthew 14:16-20; Matthew 15:32-37; Luke 24:41-43.
4. Romans 8:38-39.
5. 1 Corinthians 6:19-20.
6. Romans 5:8.

CHAPTER 9: THIS LITTLE SHAME OF MINE

1. Jeremiah 17:9, NIV.
2. Isaiah 43:18-19; Romans 8:1; 2 Corinthians 5:17; 1 John 1:9; Psalm 103:12.

CHAPTER 10: TRUE WHOLENESS WAITS

1. 2 Corinthians 5:21.

About the Author

KRISTEN LAVALLEY is a writer and storyteller whose words offer a refreshing perspective on faith and spirituality. She is the author of *Even If He Doesn't* and regularly shares insights that intersect doubt and belief, hope and suffering, beauty and heartache. With a deep love for the Christian faith and a willingness to explore its complexities, Kristen offers nuanced conversations that challenge readers to think deeply and wrestle with important questions. Kristen lives in Massachusetts with her husband, Zach, and their five children.